1975

This book may be kept

FOURTEEN DAYS

A fine will be charged for each day the book is kept overtime.

GAYLORD 142			PRINTED IN U.S.A.

PLAYS, POLITICS, AND POLEMICS

PLAYS, POLITICS, AND POLEMICS

Catharine Hughes

Drama Book Specialists/Publishers
New York

DRAMA BOOK SPECIALISTS/PUBLISHERS, 150 West 52nd Street, New York, New York 10019

Library of Congress Catalog Card Number: 72-90201
ISBN: 0-910482-43-8

Library of Congress Cataloging in Publication Data

Hughes, Catharine, 1935-
    Plays, politics, and polemics.

    Bibliography: p.
    1. Drama—20th century—History and criticism. 2. Politics in literature.
I. Title.
PN1861.H83   809.2'04   72-90201   ISBN 0-910482-43-8

For
Father Thomas F. Carey,
O.P. (1904-1972), of the
Blackfriars Guild

The thing is not necessarily either true or false; it can be both true and false.

—Harold Pinter

CONTENTS

INTRODUCTION

A few seasons ago, the Museum of Modern Art sponsored an exhibition called "The Artist as Adversary," which prompted John Canaday to remark in *The New York Times*: "The rule even seems to have become that the more worthy the cause, the worse the art." The situation is hardly confined to art. Almost from the first, plays of political or social protest, plays in the theatre of controversy, have been subject to the same accusation. And more often than not have been guilty.

Nietzsche suggested that convictions are prisons, which exclude from life the fun of doubt and flexibility. A good case could be made for the contention that, while an Ibsen or a Shaw may in a sense rise above his convictions—another way of saying, not be shackled by them—lesser artists are seldom so fortunate. Lacking the genius, or perhaps merely the vision, to transform their protest into art, they too often speak only to the converted—speaking with the clichés, the catchwords, and the oversimplifications of the propagandist rather than with the power of illumination possessed by the true creative artist, the truly creative work.

Whether or not any of this matters in the long run is open to question. The "protest" plays of the committed dramatists of the past that have endured have done so because they prompt our response to a character more than to a cause. Although supporters of Women's Lib were much in evidence at a recent Off Broadway revival of *A Doll's House*, it is Nora's secret, her concealed forgery, and what it does to her and to her marriage, not any suffragist polemic, that continues to lend the play its poignance and power. Ibsen may have felt impelled to protest the role of women in society; he also seems to have regretted the play being taken by some for a militant feminist position paper.

It is true, of course, that a playwright may on occasion set out to write a piece of propaganda, to advance a cause or denounce a wrong, and, almost accidentally, create a work of art. A few of the plays discussed in the pages that follow succeed in doing so. More do not. That does not necessarily mean they fail.

But, to get back to the question—does it matter, matter politically, that is? Do we overestimate the influence of art, attribute to it a potential for effect, a role in bringing about change, that in reality it does not possess? Does, for instance, Aleksandr Solzhenitsyn's *August 1914* have a political effect in itself or only in the fact that it is not possible for the Russian people to read something we ourselves have ready access to?

Do, for that matter, plays like *The Deputy*, *Vietnam Discourse*, or *Inquest*, passionately committed political plays, ever change anything—even, perhaps most of all, men's minds? To ask a final question: Was Brecht effective as a political force *through his writings* or as a name that could be employed—and exploited—by East Germany at a time when it had so little else to adorn it? A state may lend prestige to an artist; an artist may pay lip or more wholehearted service to a state. Yet, how often does his work, his actual work, really count politically?

Obviously, it sometimes does. Not because it brings about immediate change, not because it rights wrongs, but because it causes men to think. And it is only when they think that change becomes possible.

Although all plays in the theatre of controversy are in a sense protest plays—expressions of discontent over a situation, an action, or a failure to act—many are as interested in revelation as in alteration. Heinar Kipphardt's *In the Matter of J. Robert Oppenheimer* does not seek to rectify, even to protest a fact, so much as it seeks to reveal a state of mind that exists to this day, if in more sophisticated forms. Rolf Hochhuth's *The Deputy* and *Soldiers* are concerned not merely with indictments of expediency, but with a plea for men to apprehend the nature of individual responsibility. Daniel Berrigan's *The Trial of the Catonsville Nine* is not simply a protest against the Vietnam War, but a plea that conscience is *not* irrelevant—even though it has been ruled irrelevant in an American court of law and men have gone to prison for it.

It is plays like *The Deputy* and *Soldiers*, like Conor Cruise O'Brien's *Murderous Angels* and Donald Freed's *Inquest*, that raise some of the major questions concerning, and at times almost invalidating, that branch of the theatre of controversy known as the theatre of fact. The major one, of course, is the playwright's responsibility to history, a responsibility that carries with it an obligation to an audience that is unlikely to be as conversant with the "facts" as the playwright and hence unaware of the process of selection it is being exposed to, of what is historically valid and what is the purest supposition or, on occasion, outright distortion.

In reality, a theatre of fact probably borders on the impossible; it implies presenting all sides, showing not the black or white of a situation, but that far more difficult theatrical color—gray. If the truth is not wholly contained in the facts, and the facts do not necessarily communicate the truth, it remains a fact that theatre based on the appeal to a higher truth—which permits ignoring facts or treating them irresponsibly—is probably best given the label it deserves: theatre of propaganda. There is nothing wrong with propaganda. There is, however, something wrong, at least something that is a cause for uneasiness, about its misrepresentation, especially when that misrepresentation involves the elaborate use of news films, court transcripts, sound tracks, and the other technical devices now available to the theatre. They have a life of their own, a reality that too often serves to cloak fiction with the mantle of fact. Far too often, they result in plays that are disingenuous, plays that are cheating.

Although a Hochhuth or an O'Brien may accurately point out that his introductions or appendixes indicate the areas where he has crossed from the historical to the hypothetical, from the theatre of fact to the theatre of fiction, the audience is unlikely to be familiar with the printed text of the play (which, in any case, may not be available at the time of the production) or with its sources, "sidelights on history," or the other paraphernalia that might provide an insight into just what liberties have been taken. There is a temptation to accept documentary drama as we once accepted the old "March of Time" films—to accept as documentary what is being offered as documentary—rather than to view it as what it is: another man's view of truth.

It is the very fact that they do cheat that most frequently causes such plays to fail both as theatre and as polemic. The stacked deck is inherently undramatic. It denies the very confrontation that brings the antagonists—whether individuals or ideas—into focus, the confrontation that permits the audience to make up its own mind.

In what Walter Kerr calls the "contest between fact and imagination," it is almost inevitable that neither will win. When Hochhuth referred, in his "Sidelights on History" in *The Deputy*, to his effort to "intuitively combine the already available facts into a truthful whole," he suggested the problem. Used together in the same work, fact and fiction, documentation and imagination, tend to subvert each other. "The introduction of imagination corrupts the purity of the factual basis," writes Kerr. "The insistence upon factuality impedes imagination." A play such as Stanley R. Greenberg's *Pueblo*, which is much more "factual" than most plays in the theatre of fact, typifies the dilemma. When deprived of the admittedly risky act of the imagination that might take the playwright inside the heart and mind of Commander Lloyd Bucher, it becomes nothing more than a dramatization of what is already widely known.

Peter Weiss has Hoderer, a character in his 1962 novel *Fluchtpunkt*, say: "You can interpret all art just as you please, but you'll only be asked one question: 'What side are you on?'" Can political theatre, whether topical or historical, be both "true" and true to itself, to the "side" it is on? Can it, in effect, serve two masters? Arthur Miller has written: "I do not believe that any work of art can help but be diminished by its adherence at any cost to a political program, including its author's, and not for any other reason than there is no political program—any more than there is a theory of tragedy—which can encompass the complexities of life."

xiv

It is those complexities that the political play too often is forced—or feels called upon—to deny. That is its major weakness, and an oddly unnecessary one. Looking at the plays that have been written about the Vietnam War, it is difficult to think of one that would not have been strengthened by the admission that those who led America into it were not unregenerate villains, but men who, regardless of their public certitude, experienced doubts. "Of all things certain," says Brecht, "the most certain is doubt." Without that admission of doubt, the playwright almost inevitably speaks only to those already of the faith, reenforcing the certainties of the converted, but abdicating the possibility of persuading those who indeed may be in doubt, who may be willing to listen to reason if not to blatant polemic.

"Without continual freedom of choice," says Rolf Hochhuth, "there can be no dramatic conflict." That is the problem faced by most plays in the theatre of controversy.

"Soldiers" originally appeared, in somewhat different form, under the title "Hochhuth's Morality Play" in *America*, June 8, 1968, and is reprinted here with its permission. Portions of several other chapters originally appeared in *Plays and Players*.

PLAYS, POLITICS, AND POLEMICS

PART ONE:
AMERICA HURRAH?

Are you so liberal that you
can't think of anything better
to do for a cause than lose it?

Feiffer's America

Jules Feiffer's America, like the real one, is a risky place to live. People are afraid to walk its streets; they kill and are killed on a moment's whim in a random act of violence. They stage civil wars, then don't know what to do with them. They murder in the White House as readily as they murder in an Asian or a South American jungle. No one would call it a nice place to visit, even less a nice place to live.

"Satire is an attempt to get at the root of a situation and expose it by the extension of logic," says Feiffer. "By taking it to the point where it might become ridiculous, certain truths about situations can be revealed."* *Little Murders*, *God Bless*, and *The White House Murder Case* each show a working out of this theory against the background of contemporary American society (or, in the case of *God Bless*, American society in the immediate future). None is wholly successful, yet none—including the much-maligned *God Bless*—can be ignored by anyone concerned with political theatre in America. In displaying his antagonism toward the System, his distrust of both Right and Left, Feiffer, satirist and creator of a cartoon-America, is one of the most valuable and incisive observers we have.

*Jules Feiffer, "Talking to John Lahr," *Transatlantic Review* 32 (Summer 1969).

Little Murders, which Feiffer calls a "post-assassination play," is set in a New York where there are two double-locks on every apartment door, where the ringing of the phone is as likely to herald the "Breather" as the friend, electrical black-outs are a way of life, and gunfire in the streets is at most a matter for passing curiosity. It is a time and a place ripe for riposte, and Feiffer's lance goes at it with vigor and venom.

The Newquists—or at least three of them: Marjorie and Carol, both in their fifties, and their son, Kenny, who is in his early twenties—live in a typical Upper West Side apartment. As the play opens, they are awaiting the arrival of their daughter, Patsy, and Alfred, who wants to marry her. Carol is, to say the least, apprehensive. Patsy draws homosexuals "like flies. . . . She's got *too much stuff*" for "real men." But when they arrive, it doesn't turn out that way. Patsy is still Patsy: tall, blond, vibrant, the all-American girl; but Alfred is, well, Alfred: large, phlegmatic, and dour, with two cameras, the tools of his trade, hung around his neck. He has his "usual assortment of bruises," remnants of the fact that he gets beat up at least once a week. "There are," he says, "lots of little people who like to start fights with big people. They hit me for a couple of minutes, they see I'm not going to fall down, they get tired and they go away."

Alfred, it seems, is an "apathist." So long as his cameras are left alone, he doesn't mind being beat up. Besides, it has been going on for ten years and he has yet to get knocked uncon-scious. It's hardly the stance Patsy would take—not Patsy, the former tomboy and cheerleader, with her spirit and her exuber-ance, her get-up-and-go. No, Patsy, the archetypical American, would hardly put up with such nonsense. Self-doubt is alien to her. Like the America that spawned her, she knows herself to be right in every instance; she believes, as Feiffer wrote to the director of the Royal Shakespeare Company's production, "in initiative, resourcefulness, home, the family, God, motherhood, and country." She is optimistic to the point of blindness; she is positive, logical, and secure. And, when she dies, part of America dies.

But Patsy, eager, aggressive, even appealing, is also twenty-seven. The "right men" all got married two years ago and she

4

gets "migraine from being so damnably dependable." She is tired of being Mother Earth. That is why she is so attracted to Alfred: he's the only man she knows who isn't waiting for her to "save" him. And so, of course, save him she must, whether from himself or from the muggers he meets on the street. But Alfred doesn't really want to be saved; he's quite content as he is. Once he was a commercial photographer working for *Holiday* and *Esquire* and *Vogue*. Now, he takes pictures of shit: "I've been shooting shit for a year now, and I've already won a half-dozen awards." Obviously, he poses a major reclamation job for Patsy, and at the moment she isn't succeeding: "He doesn't know how to fight; *that's* why I'm not winning."

When the time comes for their wedding, there is another problem: Alfred doesn't want God in the ceremony. That rules out the Newquists' minister; it also, as it turns out, rules out Carol's good friend the judge. Ethical Culture is willing, but Ethical Culture has to have ethical culture in the ceremony. That's out too. Eventually, they get around to the Reverend Dupas, pastor of the First Existential Church in Greenwich Village. Of the two hundred marriages he has performed, all but seven have failed. It's easy to see why.

> DUPAS: Failing one's partner does *not* matter. Nothing can hurt if we do not see it as hurtful. Nothing can destroy if we will not see it as destructive. It is all part of life. . . . So now, Alfred. Do you take Patricia as your lawfully wedded wife, to love—whatever *that* means—to honor—but is not dishonor, in a sense, a *form* of honor? to keep her in sickness, in health, in prosperity and adversity—what nonsense!—Forsaking all others—what a shocking invasion of privacy! . . . as long as you both shall live—or as long as you're not bored with each other?

Feiffer's wedding ceremony is a superb set-piece, a deft, brilliantly observed parody of existential freedom carried to an extreme that turns it into a straitjacket. In a world where everything is "all right," nothing has meaning.

5

Act 2 turns the tables. The violence that has been lurking outside—in the gunshots, the sirens, the muggings, the depraved voice on the telephone—enters the Newquist apartment. The hysteria that has been just beneath the surface erupts. Middle-class fears give way to middle-class murders and murderers. What Feiffer has called "the Andy Hardy family," living for decades with a cold war morality, warped by the violence of Vietnam, the violence of poverty and discrimination, has its comfortable mythology shattered; it, too, turns violent.

It only seems to begin with the gunshot that shatters the apartment window and leaves Patsy dead on the floor. This occurs just after Alfred has told her, "Yes, Patsy—I'm going to feel." Her all-American reclamation program has taken its first tentative step. Patsy has convinced him—perhaps "convinced" is too strong a word—that there may be another way, her way. Perhaps life is not "shit" after all. With Patsy dead at his feet, it is a thought Alfred must cling to.

And cling to it he does, becoming in the last scene a surrogate for Patsy in the life of the Newquists, taking photographs not of shit but of Patsy, photographs of photographs that become huge blowups of her eyes, nose, hair, lips, teeth. Alfred is happy—very likely he is also mad—as he goes about his work to the sound of gunfire in the streets.

It is six months later and now there are four different locks and bolts on the door. Carol returns from making deliveries of the photographs. The "Patsy series" is selling like hotcakes, but he has come from a stop at police headquarters, where he has been shot in the leg: "It was my own dammed fault. I didn't give the password." There have been 345 unsolved murders in the past six months. "There's got be be a conspiracy."

Carol notices that Alfred has a black eye. Alfred's role reversal is complete: a kid was staring at him in the park, so he "beat the crap out of him." It was his fourth fight this week, but he's still ready to "go a couple of quick ones" with Carol. Carol demurs. As Marjorie says a moment later, they get shot at every day. There has just been a new murder in the building—she doesn't know who: "It's in the other wing." She has invited Lieutenant Practice to join them for coffee as soon as he has

6

finished investigating. Practice may not have a solution for the murders, but he does have a theory:

> Who has the most to gain? People in high places. Their names would astound you. People in low places. Concealing their activities beneath a cloak of poverty. People in all walks of life. Left wing and right wing. Black and white. Students and scholars. A conspiracy of such ominous proportions that we may not know the whole truth in our lifetime, and we will never be able to reveal all the facts. We are readying mass arrests.

Which would seem to allow for most contingencies.

Carol, meanwhile, has had about all he can take. His side needs weapons too. They have to train. "It's freedom I'm talking about!" he shouts. "There's a fox loose in the chicken coop! *Kill him!* I want my *freedom!*"

Easier done than said, as it turns out, for the Newquists by now have a rifle stashed away beneath the couch. A few moments later, they are taking turns shooting at passersby from the window. It's a new parlor game: "Why don't you try *your* luck?" Carol asks Alfred. And they do, all of them, as Marjorie wheels in a serving cart with drinks and lights the candles on the dining-room table. It is, after all, "nice to have [her] family laughing again."

Feiffer's America is a nation of paradoxes. Clean-cut, short-haired representatives of the middle class become killers; long-haired militants stage revolutions only to join the Establishment; the grisly becomes the hilarious; a seemingly obvious occasion for satire provides the setting for events of deep-seated political and moral ambiguity. Sanity is only a step from insanity, the Right only another face of the Left, violence only another face of fear. It is, as Feiffer has said, an America that "is literally up for grabs."

And, as *God Bless* tries to show with only sputtering success, everyone is willing to do his share of the grabbing.

William Clark Brackman was fourteen years old when he led the miners out on strike. Now he is one hundred and ten.

Although the nation is in turmoil, it still honors its revered elder statesman, the "great dissenter" and adviser to presidents. He is a legend in his own lifetime—admittedly easier if one lives to one hundred and ten. *Time, Life, Newsweek,* and *The Progressive* have done cover stories on him in the same week, and now it is the turn of "the radical Catholic weekly" *American Heretic* to give him his due. He is in the midst of taping an interview with Father Whiting—an interview in which he acknowledges: "For the first ninety years of my life I was an idealist. Twenty years ago. . . I converted to cynicism." A phone call comes. His wife, Eve, takes the message: they may soon be hearing gunfire for there is "some trouble at the Washington Monument." In the background, through the window of Brackman's Georgetown home, the monument may be seen to tremble slightly, then to shudder.

"The President has declared a state of martial law," Eve tells them, and Brackman is soon to receive "an important visitor." In the meantime, however, they can continue with the interview. Brackman tells Whiting of his role as a labor leader, as an adviser to presidents from Grover Cleveland to Lyndon Johnson. His story is anything but one of consistent idealism. Indeed, it prompts Whiting to suggest:

> Sir, you are known as a great humanitarian, a great civil libertarian, a great liberal. Yet as you describe your early years they seem to be made up of every conceivable sort of compromise . . . and, I hope I don't put this too strongly. . . betrayal. How do you reconcile this seeming contradiction between principle and practice?

But Brackman has fallen asleep and doesn't wake up until Ames and Norman RX arrive. They are both in their late twenties and his former students at Harvard. They are heavily armed. The ALF—the American Liberation Front—is "overthrowing the fascists," they declare. A loud explosion is heard and the Washington Monument slowly topples.

There are riots in forty-six cities. The ALF has possession of every B-52 on the eastern seaboard. But the ALF wants

Brackman's support. There is an Asian war and an African war and a Latin American war. Brackman is unimpressed with their rhetoric, their thrust for power. They are bound to be disappointed. Power "doesn't even corrupt anymore, it disables," he tells them.

Ames and RX disagree. They will wait for the president to arrive. Meanwhile, they hurl some more revolutionary rhetoric and, when Brackman again falls asleep, they argue over which of them gave up Eve to him. Each, it seems, has been her lover. Father Whiting and Eve also go at it. Whiting is disillusioned over Brackman's compromises, his "twists and turns." Eve, on the other hand, challenges: "Are you so liberal that you can't think of anything better to do for a cause than lose it?"

Finally, the president arrives. He is, he admits, "in trouble." And why?

> Who organized and financed this whole abysmal operation? . . . It was purely and simply a clever, allegedly well-organized tactic instigated by your President . . . your President . . . and carried out by a trusted undercover squad of top level government infiltrators into the peace and black extremist movements.

Now, however, things have gotten out of hand. It could "very well be the death knell of liberalism as we know it in this country," the president tells them. And all because Ames and RX fell down on the job he was paying them for. Once the riots are put down, he warns, there will be a right-wing backlash; there will be detention camps, a reactionary secret police, and a fascist junta. When the House Un-American Activities Committee finds out the administration funded the riots, he'll be impeached. Ames and RX are unimpressed; they merely find it the occasion for more militant rhetoric.

> PRESIDENT: I've got half a mind to surrender the government to you at that. Then it could be my turn to dissent. But I wouldn't be extended that privilege would I? I'd probably be shot.

9

"Why is it always such an effort to find out what you people are for?" he demands. Ames and RX may not be *for* anything, but they do have plans that include revoking the Constitution, abolishing Congress, murdering the eldest male white child in every middle-class family in America, and bombing one city a week for an entire year. "We will take violence off the television screens and bring it into the homes," they assert. As for the president, he is their prisoner.

Brackman, sage that he is, decides the time has come to negotiate. "If the situation is not to deteriorate into civil war and anarchy the President must appear on television within the hour and announce the formation of a caretaker coalition government." But they can't even agree on *who* is to go on television. Brackman suggests all three appear. They continue to disagree; to bargain over cities to be bombed and whether to give the bomb to black extremists, and the like. They are, however, united on one thing: the wars must end. We must surrender. Archetypical naive liberal that he is, Father Whiting is stunned by what he is hearing. "You murdered my country," he shouts, pointing a gun at them. Then he collapses, dead of "mind failure," says Brackman. "He died of inflexibility," he explains. The president, Ames, and RX head for the television studio.

There are both witty and wise moments in *God Bless;* observations that are pertinent and perceptive. But there are really two currents at work—that of Brackman and his compromises and that of the events of the moment—and they are never really fused into a cohesive dramatic event. The play is at times as woolly-minded as the type of liberalism it scorns.

What, in fact, does Feiffer actually want to say? That pragmatic liberalism has failed? That when victims become victors they have their own victims and it is only a question of which side you're on? That compromise and cynicism are the only way? At one time or another he says all of these, says them with a redundancy that begins to try the patience. They are hardly new observations; certainly they are not new insights. Yet they seldom move *beyond* observations. Feiffer brings wit but no real point of view to them—at least no consistent point of view.

10

He has defended himself by saying: "What's being said is that if I don't pick from labels A, B, C, and D, then I haven't picked anything. I don't think those are the only choices. I don't really think the choice is between Lyndon Johnson and Abbie Hoffman." At the same time, he insists that the liberal mentality Brackman represents, the mentality that elects to be "effective" rather than idealistic, is exactly the kind of "effectiveness [that] has brought the U.S. to many betrayals, one of which is Vietnam."

All very well, but it is a statement after the fact, not a fact implicit in the play. The play meanders about in search of just such a focus, only to obfuscate at every turn. If the question concerning Feiffer's militants is what are they "for," the same might be said of Feiffer himself in his ambiguous relationship to his material. Ambivalence and satire make uncomfortable allies.

So, on occasion, do dichotomy and satire. When *The White House Murder Case* opened Off Broadway in 1970, Feiffer drew a cartoon for the program and advertising. It showed a soldier in helmet and combat boots impaled by a picket sign bearing the title. About midway through the play itself, the white mini-skirted wife of the president is found stretched out on a conference table impaled by a picket sign proclaiming "Make Love, Not War." Why a soldier in one case and the First Lady in the other? It really couldn't matter less, of course (the soldier doubtless worked better in the ads), but it does suggest a similar dichotomy within the play itself.

As in *God Bless* and *Little Murders*, Feiffer has latched on to an arresting idea for scathing, pertinent satire, only to let his imagination lead him down a path or two too many. We're in Brazil this time (the American Army does get around) and in the White House, and, using blackouts, Feiffer cuts from one to the other to unfold his caustic, sometimes very funny little saga. It seems someone has inadvertently employed an experimental nerve gas called CB 97, and the CB 97, normally "an effective weapon in our peace arsenal," has blown the wrong way, killing 750 Americans and disabling a good many more. ("What are American troops doing down on their knees in front of a bunch of goddam Brazilians?" demands their commander.)

11

All this creates a bit of understandable consternation at the White House, since "six weeks before a presidential election isn't the time to try out poison gas." The secretary of defense, attorney general, postmaster general (who is also the party chairman), and presidential science adviser rally round the president to try to figure out what to tell the American people. To compound things, the president's wife is murdered while everyone is out of the room drawing up lists of newspapermen likely to be cooperative in spreading the administration version of who was responsible for the ill-timed accident. It winds up "a suicide squad of Brazilian terrorists."

But who's responsible for the murder of the First Lady— peace groups, the blacks, the opposition? Hardly. The fingerprints of the president and the attorney general are on the weapon (but the weapon *is* the broken shaft of a golf club). It turns out, however, to be the postmaster general, who is convinced that "what's good for the Party is good for the country." He wants a voice in foreign policy and . . . Things go on like that for a while, as the guardians of the American destiny now have to figure out what to tell the American people about the First Lady's death as well (*that* is blamed on food poisoning in Chicago).

Meanwhile, Feiffer regularly cuts back to the battlefield, where two soldiers are beginning to feel the increasing effects of CB 97. As their extremities drop off one by one, they think beautiful thoughts (on their nerve-gas high) and come to all forms of idealistic conclusions about Love, Understanding, and the ultimate destiny of mankind (more Love). Until, that is, the soldier responsible for the "accident" in the first place exultantly realizes he may have gotten some Brazilians too. He has balls, after all! So much for love and understanding.

The White House Murder Case has some marvelous moments and some grisly ones. There is a scene in which the secretary of defense, multicolored maps and diagrams flying, glosses over the latest defeat in Brazil ("There have been setbacks, and 'Operation Total Win' was one of them") in a Pentagonese of chilling rightness, and Feiffer's caustic swipes at official hypocrisy and cynicism and the extent to which the violence is always greener on the other side of the ocean are often deft and

12

savagely pertinent. But, somehow, despite his intelligence and concern, the pieces never quite come together into a sustained piece of theatre. There are too many inconsistencies in style and tone, too much diffusion of focus, too much obvious puppetry. As he has demonstrated in each of his plays, Feiffer *knows*; he's right about where we're wrong. But he writes with the hand of the cartoonist—with the ability to communicate an image—rather than with the ability to pursue and expand his insights into true perceptions that speak beyond the moment. It is this that makes him at the same time one of the most fascinating and one of the most exasperating dramatists writing today.

*Is the accuser always holy
now? Were they born this
morning as clean as God's
fingers?*

The Crucible

"The community at large had become bewitched . . . bewitched
by a kind of mad hypnosis, expressed in panic on the one hand
and crusading fervour on the other. At such moments the voice
of reason always sounds like blasphemy and dissenters are of
the devil."* "Such moments" have, of course, occurred countless times in history: the Salem witch trials of which Marion
Starkey was writing; the time of the earlier diabolical possession
of which Huxley wrote in *The Devils of Loudun* and John Whiting in *The Devils*; the nationalist hysteria that captured the German *Volk* during the artificial festivity of Hitler's Nuremberg
rallies in the 30s; and, of course, the more recent witch hunts of
the McCarthy period in postwar America.

It is this, not simply its obvious and acknowledged genesis in
McCarthyism, that today lends Arthur Miller's *The Crucible*
much of its fascination. For, as Miss Starkey notes, the story of
Salem in 1692 is "an allegory of our times."

*Marion L. Starkey, *The Devil in Massachusetts: A Modern Enquiry
into the Salem Witch Trials* (Garden City, N.Y.: Doubleday, Anchor
Books, 1969), p. 102.

When *The Crucible* was first produced in January, 1953, it was almost impossible to view it outside the context of the events that had impelled Miller to write it. Although it is hardly necessary to agree with Brooks Atkinson's assertion that it "met McCarthyism head-on"—the truth is a bit more oblique—it is unlikely the play would have been written without the impetus provided by the junior senator from Wisconsin, though Miller himself did not run afoul of Congress until 1956, when he was cited for contempt for his refusal to name those who had attended a Communist writers' meeting eight years earlier.

Because Miller does stretch and alter facts in the pursuit of his analogy, the consideration of the play as a reflection of *its* time remains valid (at least I intend to employ it), provided one keeps in mind that, while "demons" may not always be among us, mass psychosis and at least the potential for institutionalized political and social hysteria almost invariably are. A fair summary might be Miller's own, in 1965: "McCarthyism may have been the historical occasion of the play, not its theme."

Perhaps because he is dealing with figures whose lives prior to and even after the Salem witch trials are little documented, in some cases virtually unknown, and certainly without the massive implications of the actions of a Churchill (in *Soldiers*), a Pius XII (in *The Deputy*), or a Hammarskjöld (in *Murderous Angels*), there is an inclination to give Miller more of the benefit of the doubt than is the case with, say, Rolf Hochhuth or Conor Cruise O'Brien. Otherwise, it would be necessary to point out that a single fact, among many others—the raising of Abigail Williams's age from its actual eleven to *The Crucible*'s seventeen in order to permit the adultery that is the play's fulcrum—would almost totally invalidate the play as "history." What Miller has attempted—apart from his analogy with the temperament of the 50s—is to convey the "essential nature" of the time. With that in mind, I see little reason not to give him that benefit of the doubt.

When the play opens, the first whispers (soon to be shouts) of witchcraft already are being heard in Salem. Betty Parris, the ten-year-old daughter of the Reverend Samuel Parris, a widower and minister of the Salem Village parish since 1689, has been mysteriously afflicted. She lies abed, her eyes closed, perhaps ill—or so Parris must by now be beginning to hope—perhaps under the influence of some otherworldly spell evoked by Tituba, his Negro slave from Barbados. His niece, Abigail Williams, enters with her friend Susanna Walcott. They confirm, or at least begin to confirm, his worst fears: the doctor "cannot discover no medicine for it in his books." Susanna goes on to tell him, "He have been searchin' his books since he left you, sir. But he bid me tell you, that you might look to unnatural things for the cause of it."

Parris is appalled; he refuses to accept it. Surely the Reverend John Hale—a man who, after all, is a specialist in such things and is on his way from Beverly—will confirm that "there be no unnatural cause here." Not under *his* roof, not at a time when "there is a faction that is sworn to drive me from my pulpit."

But Parris knows that there is *something* afoot, that Betty is suffering from something more than a bad cold or some familiar childhood ailment. She has not been able to "move herself" since midnight. Besides, he has seen her and his niece "dancing like heathen" in the forest. At first, but only at first, Abigail's explanation is simple enough:

> Uncle, we did dance; let you tell them I confessed it—and I'll be whipped if I must be. But they're speakin' of witchcraft. Betty's not witched. . . . When you leaped out of the bush so suddenly, Betty was frightened and then she fainted. And there's the whole of it.

But Parris thinks he saw more than just dancing: Tituba waving her arms over the fire and screeching "gibberish," a dress lying on the grass, and—perhaps the ultimate horror for a Puritan—someone running naked through the trees.

Abigail is terrified, but she swears that no one was naked, that "there is nothin' more." Parris is not altogether convinced. "Your name in the town," he asks, "it is entirely white, is it not?"

> ABIGAIL: Why, I am sure that it is, sir. There be no blush about my name.

17

PARRIS: Abigail, is there any other cause than you have told me, for your being discharged from Goody Proctor's service? I have heard it said . . . that she comes so rarely to the church this year for she will not sit so close to something soiled. What signified that remark?

ABIGAIL: She hates me, uncle, she must, for I would not be her slave. It's a bitter woman, a lying, cold, sniveling woman, and I will not work for such a woman.

As it turns out, well might Elizabeth Proctor hate the young and dissembling Abby. But, before the reasons are revealed, other of the Salem Village girls than Betty will be afflicted. Ruth Putnam, daughter of one of its most influential families, is the first of them. When it is reported, Abby, eighteen-year-old Mercy Lewis, and seventeen-year-old Mary Warren, Proctor's servant, two of the other nocturnal dancers, begin to panic: "They'll be callin' us witches." Perhaps it will even come out that, as Betty says when the girls are alone, Abby drank blood, "drank a charm to kill John Proctor's wife."

But before Abby can finish warning them not to speak further of it, John Proctor himself enters. He is a farmer in his middle thirties. Mary flees, frightened at the wrath Proctor displays over her failure to observe his instructions not to leave the house. John and Abby are left alone with the seemingly unconscious Betty. "She took fright, is all," Abby insists. She pleads with him for a "soft word"; she has been waiting for him every night:

I know how you clutched my back behind your house and sweated like a stallion whenever I come near! Or did I dream that? It's she put me out, you cannot pretend it were you. I saw your face when she put me out, and you loved me then and you do now.

By the time the Reverend John Hale arrives, their emotions have risen to a higher pitch. Hale is about forty, an intellectual. With his heavy tomes on witchcraft, his command of its symp-

18

toms, and his means of diagnosis, his first warning to them is reassuring: "We cannot look to superstition in this. The Devil is precise." He examines Betty and when he hears of the dancing in the forest and the attendant activities, he asks Abigail if she called the Devil.

Abby is frightened. Trying to save herself from punishment, she bursts out that it was Tituba who called the Devil, that Tituba made both her and Betty do it. Then she adds, "She makes me drink blood!" Now she is carried away: not only did Tituba call on the Devil, not only did she make her drink blood, but she has caused her to "laugh at prayer" and dream "corruptions."

Even more terrified than her accuser, Tituba says, "I do believe somebody else be witchin' these children . . . the Devil got him numerous witches." Eventually, Tituba confesses whom *she* has seen with him. There was Goody Good, and, yes, Goody Osburn. Her confession unleashes the floodgates—and the imaginations—first of Abigail, then of little Betty. Their "crying-out" becomes ever more ecstatic, its reception ever more joyous.

Not, of course, in all quarters. At the Proctors, for instance, there is apprehension. Elizabeth is suspicious, for she has not forgotten what occurred between Abby and John seven months before. And she will not let *him* forget it. "You forget nothin' and forgive nothin'," he says when she attacks him for having been alone with Abby on the day of the crying-out. "I cannot speak but I am doubted, every moment judged for lies, as though I come into a court when I come into this house!"

Their quarrel is broken off when Mary Warren returns from the court, where, she says, she is now an "official." She comes with some bad news: thirty-nine women have now been arrested and today Elizabeth has been "somewhat mentioned." But she brings something besides news: a poppet she has made for Elizabeth.

Although Mary will not say, Elizabeth knows who has accused her. It is Abby, and "she thinks to kill me, then to take my place." She pleads with John to go to Abby to break "whatever promise she may sense."

But too many wheels already have been set in motion; too

19

many influential figures are involved. Some already have been sentenced or have confessed. Too many reputations are now at stake. Besides, says Hale to Francis Nurse, whose wife has been taken,

> these are new times, sir. There is a misty plot afoot so subtle we should be criminal to cling to old respects and ancient friendships. . . . The Devil is alive in Salem, and we dare not quail to follow wherever the accusing finger points!

Among those it points to is Elizabeth. The evidence? The very poppet given to her by Mary Warren, with a needle plunged into it. Abby had warned them only hours before: Elizabeth's "familiar spirit" had pushed a needle into her. Elizabeth is taken away. Why, Proctor demands, is it Abigail or Parris who is to be believed? "Is the accuser always holy now? Were they born this morning as clean as God's fingers?"

Hale is deeply disturbed. Although he has been party to unleashing the hysteria of Salem Village, he has begun to feel uncertain, even guilty, over some of the things he has seen, over some of the respected and apparently virtuous citizens who have been taken into custody. Might it be, as Proctor suggests, that "vengeance is walking Salem"?

If Hale is not yet ready to act, Proctor is: he will take Mary Warren to court and, he says, Mary will tell the court all she knows.

Though Hale is potentially the most complex and interesting character in the play, Miller regrettably never lets him become so. It is he who, in time, really will be torn by doubt, forced to a change of mind that the others never confront in their various certainties, grievances, and acts of cunning and duplicity. Instead, Miller elects to concentrate on the emotional triangle of John, Elizabeth, and Abby.

A short time before the Broadway production of the play closed, Miller added a new scene at this point. Though designed to reenforce the relationship between John and Abby, it in fact acts more as a deterrent to the play's forward momentum than anything else. They meet in the wood and Abby, seemingly bordering on madness, professes her continuing love: "Oh, John, I will make you such a wife when the world is white again! You will be amazed to see me every day, a light of heaven in your house."

John will have none of it. He has come to warn Abby that his wife goes to trial the next day and that if Abby does not speak in a way that will free Elizabeth, she herself will be ruined. He will reveal that Abby had Mary stab the needle into the poppet:

> You will tell the court you are blind to spirits; you cannot see them any more, and you will never cry witchery again, or I will make you famous for the whore you are!

That Abby will do nothing of the kind is foreordained.

Act 3 takes place in the vestry room of the Salem meeting-house. Judge Hathorne is there, and Deputy Governor Danforth, and Francis Nurse and Giles Corey, husbands of two of the accused. Proctor brings Mary Warren before them and Mary admits of the original denunciations, the testimony, all the rest: "It were pretense, sir."

In one of the more obvious attempts at an analogy with the McCarthy era, Miller has Hale tell Danforth: "There is a prodigious fear of the court in the country. . . ."

> DANFORTH: Then there is a prodigious guilt in the country. . . . Reproach me not with the fear in the country; there is fear in the country because there is a moving plot to topple Christ in the country!
>
> HALE: But it does not follow that everyone accused is part of it.

But Danforth and Hathorne, like the village, are in too deep to admit to Hale's implications. So John takes his remaining chance: he will admit to adultery in the hope they will realize that what has taken place has been a "whore's vengeance."

Even that is not to work. His wife must be put to the test. John maintains that "she have never lied." If that is so, then she will have to admit that she put Abby out of her house "for a

21

harlot." She will have to confess that her husband committed lechery. When she is brought in, she, of course, cannot. As for poor, frightened Mary Warren, she is no match for the emotions that are at work. Confronted with Abby and the other girls, then herself accused by them of possessing an evil spirit, she cannot continue in her admission that it was all "pretense." She goes the other girls one better; she turns on John:

> You're the Devil's man! . . . "I'll murder you," he says, "if my wife hangs! We must go and overthrow the court," he says!

And so, John, too, is hauled away to jail. For Hale, it is the final straw. He denounces the proceedings and quits the court.

Not that it does John Proctor any good. Nor does the fact that Miller gratuitously has Parris admit that Abby and Mercy Lewis have run off with the contents of his strongbox. Things have reached the point where only a confession will save Proctor from hanging. Hale, acknowledging that there is blood on his head, begs Elizabeth to prevail upon John to confess, even though "damnation's doubled on a minister who counsels men to lie." Proctor's life, he tells her, is more precious than the principle, however glorious. Herself uncertain what she will say, she agrees to speak with him.

Proctor himself has begun to think of confession. He "cannot mount the gibbet like a saint." It would be a fraud, he tells Elizabeth. "I am no good man."

> ELIZABETH: It needs a cold wife to prompt lechery. . . . John, I counted myself so plain, so poorly made, no honest love would come to me! Suspicion kissed you when I did; I never knew how I should say my love. It were a cold house I kept! . . . Do what you will. But let none be your judge. There be no higher judge under heaven than Proctor is! Forgive me, forgive me, John—I never knew such goodness in the world!

There is a moment in which it seems he will give them the

22

confession they crave. But, no, they insist that he bear witness concerning others as well—another clear parallel with the events of the early 50s—and this he will not do. "I speak my own sins; I cannot judge another. I have no tongue for it." He has three children, he says, and "how may I teach them to walk like men in the world, and I sold my friends?" Nor will he *sign*; it is enough that he has confessed it and they have heard. He has given them his soul; they must leave him his name. As the drums roll, he goes off to hang: "I do think I see some shred of goodness in John Proctor."

The Reverend John Hale was to write, "We walked in clouds and could not see our way. And we have most cause to be humbled for error . . . which cannot be retrieved." But that was later, when the hysteria had faded and those who had survived it were picking up the pieces of their lives. Still later, when thoughts of witchcraft had gone out of fashion, men were inclined to view the time as a moment of aberration, as something that could not return. But, as Miss Starkey remarks, we too live in an age "beset by ideological 'heresies,'" and it was this that impelled Arthur Miller to write *The Crucible*.

Although "heresies"—and inquisitions—have existed in nearly every age, a retrospective look at the McCarthy era nonetheless leaves us a little incredulous at the fact that it was permitted to happen—that we permitted it to happen. Even after a war that has shown us the hollowness of so many of our once proud claims to some almost mystical special role in preserving and extending the democratic ethos, the spectre of the junior senator from Wisconsin standing before an audience in Wheeling, West Virginia, proclaiming, "While I cannot take time to name all the men in the State Department who have been named as members of the Communist Party and members of a spy ring, I have here a list of 205 that were known to the Secretary of State . . ." has an aura of unreality to it. That it was real, we know; that it could happen again, we have ample evidence. But to know is not necessarily to know why.

In the introduction to his *Collected Plays* Miller has written, "It was not only the rise of 'McCarthyism' that moved me, but something which seemed much more weird and mysterious. It was the fact that a political, objective, knowledgeable campaign

23

from the far Right was capable of creating not only a terror, but a new subjective reality, a veritable mystique which was gradually assuming even a holy resonance."

It was precisely such a mystique that sprang up and cloaked the young girls of Salem Village after the first crying-out and all during the long days of the examinations and trials. And, without doubt, it had its "holy resonance," as they dined at the tables of the mighty, were celebrated by their own, and even called to other towns to share their expertise.

Miller's concern is with the hysteria, with what he calls the "squirming, single, defined process which would show that the sin of public terror is that it divests man of conscience, of himself." This, strictly speaking, was much more a characteristic of the McCarthy period and of Miller's Salem than of the historians' Salem. But Miller does detect and adhere to a certain essential pattern in both: the absence of hard as opposed to "spectral" evidence (there *were* Communists, however; were there witches?), the use of confessed participants against the defendants, false confessions, guilt by association, motives of revenge, and mass psychosis. It is a world of heroes and villains, figures of black and figures of white (the exception being Hale). Its accusers are motivated by a drive for vengeance, by envy, by the need for self-preservation. Guilt and confession become not private questions but public virtues.

The two—the Salem trials and the postwar witch hunts—obviously are not fully analogous, but they possess sufficient parallels to provide Miller with a dramatically viable and operative metaphor. One of the major divergences comes with the emergence of John Proctor as hero. Proctor is independent, unwilling to conform to any man's idea of what he should be or what he should do. He questions some of the time-honored sanctions of New England theocracy. But he is not "without sin"; in fact, his sin almost may be said to be his undoing. This sets him apart from the others in the play; it sets him apart also from Miller's analogical theme.

As Penelope Curtis has noted, there is a shift "from the struggle of forces in a community to a private tension of

24

feeling."* It enlists the sympathy, but diffuses the theme; it attaches to the play too many of the elements of romantic melodrama. Because of love, Elizabeth lies to save her husband and thereby condemns him. It is arresting as a theatrical device but it diverts the attention from the questions at hand: What madness has captured Salem? What will be the fulcrum on which John Proctor's struggle of conscience, his struggle for his soul, will turn?

Despite this dichotomy, *The Crucible* ranks second— admittedly, a distant second—only to *Death of a Salesman* among Miller's works. It has numerous flaws—in exposition, in careless or deliberate oversimplification of character, in the too direct attempts to draw the analogy with the 50s, certainly in the melodrama. But on the stage, as opposed to the printed page, its vitality, power, and sense of moral outrage communicate with an intensity that transcends these failings. There is too little moral outrage in the theatre, at least too little in the professional theatre. That *The Crucible* still communicates it, even for audiences to whom "McCarthy" is simply a name from the past, if that, indicates that it has at least escaped the graveyard reserved for political plays whose time has passed.

The Critical Review, no. 8 (1965): 45-58.

25

How could I dream that offi-
cials of the Department of
Justice would lend themselves
to the perpetration of a com-
plete hoax. . .

Inquest

One of the tragedies of the Vietnam War, a war that so abounds in tragedy, is the fact that Americans—at least many Americans—who have lived through it probably never again will fully trust their government. Not on a civil rights bill or a highway, not on a social security or an arts appropriation, certainly not in terms of what constitutes the national interest. It is very unlikely unfair, it is perhaps unrealistic, but it is true. Donald Freed's *Inquest* suggests the moment has been a bit late in coming, that Huey Newton, Bobby Seale, and Eldridge Cleaver are the Julius and Ethel Rosenbergs of today and that "history won't give us a second chance."

Inquest is based upon the 1951 trial of the Rosenbergs. It is many things to many people, and few of them have much to do with theatre. Most Americans who admit to being over thirty have either the memories or the scars of the time. Joe McCarthy was on his throne and Roy Cohn and G. David Schine were his acolytes. Oppenheimer was declared a security risk and much of the State Department was branded disloyal. Arthur Miller wrote a play largely inspired by this climate and had to set it in seventeenth-century New England and present its witch hunt as a literal witch hunt. For the Old Left, *Inquest* is the remembrance

27

of things past, two hours of something approaching nostalgia. (One normally acerbic critic admitted, "I wept now and then in the course of it, not only for the Rosenbergs, but for some people who are still very close to me, and of course for myself."*) For the New Left it is a substantiation of their elders' moral flabbiness, compromises, and inability to act at a time when rhetoric was not enough. And, of course, a reminder that the trial of the Chicago Seven and the various Black Panther court cases are but the most recent links in a chain. It is subtitled "A Tale of Political Terror."

As theatre, *Inquest* is simply a bad play. As "theatre of fact," it is something worse, a play so slanted and wallowing in sentimentality, so without the willingness to entertain doubt—or even question—that it at times comes perilously close to partaking of the very techniques it wishes to indict.

As the audience enters the theatre, the curtain is up and eighteen varicolored panels proclaim: "Every word you will hear or see on this stage is a documented quotation from trial transcripts and original sources or a reconstruction from actual events." At first glance, a seemingly unqualified statement. "All courtroom dialogue is quoted from the transcripts of the trial," asserted the program for the New York production. But what of that phrase "reconstruction from actual events"? The program was nothing if not tendentious: "The 'Reconstructions' draw on letters and verbal reports, but they are inventions in the service of truth rather than facts." Presumptuous, perhaps, but it was reassuring to discover that someone had finally found the answer to "What is Truth?"

There is a line in Harold Pinter's *Old Times* that would seem to sum up the greater part of the case for the prosecution in *Inquest:* "There are things I remember which may never have happened but as I recall them so they take place." Whether it also sums up the reality of the evidence in the case of "The United States *versus* Julius Rosenberg, Ethel Rosenberg and Morton Sobell" is considerably more clouded. We all redefine the past in terms of the present. When it comes to an event such

*Julius Novick, "Between Came Tears," *The Village Voice*, April 30, 1970, p. 47.

28

as the Rosenberg trial—an event that so reflected the passions, hysteria, and confusion of its time—there can be no doubt that Justice Felix Frankfurter was right in saying, three days after the death of the Rosenbergs: "To be writing an opinion in a case affecting two lives after the curtain has been rung down upon them has the appearance of pathetic futility. But history also has its claims." Yes, and the theatre makes *its* demands. Getting the two into balance can be a precarious business.

Freed's estimate of the trial may be accurate; what it is not is convincing. After a prologue employed to create what he calls "the time chamber of the 1950s," with its mushroom clouds, its entertainment, sports, and political heroes and villains, and the arrest of the British scientist Klaus Fuchs, the voice of J. Edgar Hoover is heard:

> The secret of the atomic bomb has been stolen. *Find
> the thieves!* . . . In all the history of the FBI, there
> never was a more important problem than this one,
> never another case where we felt under such pressure.
> The unknown man simply had to be found.

A film shows Ethel Rosenberg's brother, David Greenglass, being taken into custody. Headlines begin to tell the story of the "atomic spy ring" and, finally, there come the films showing the arrest of Julius Rosenberg, an electrical engineer of thirty-two, and his thirty-five-year-old wife. The upstage panels display their ominous J. Edgar Hoover, a grinning, golfing President Eisenhower, and headlines from the American and foreign press; the sound track carries martial music and the pleas of the pope, Sartre, Einstein, and others. The defense attorney, Emanuel Bloch, steps forward to say: "I can't tell you what really happened to those two human beings. Let me put it to you this way—the future determines the past." (The latter words were in fact spoken by Morton Sobell after his release in 1969. Although he was tried with the Rosenbergs, Freed does not deal with this aspect of the case.)

The body of the play is set in the U.S. District Court, Southern District of New York. The jury is chosen, the grand jury indictment read, asserting the government's contention

29

that the Rosenbergs and other defendants did, "the United States then and there being at war, conspire, combine, confederate and agree with each other and with Harry Gold and Ruth Greenglass" to hand over to the Soviet Union "the most important secrets ever known to mankind." And, says U.S. Attorney Irving H. Saypol,

> the evidence will reveal to you how the Rosenbergs persuaded David Greenglass, Mrs. Rosenberg's own brother, to play the treacherous role of a modern Benedict Arnold, while wearing the uniform of the United States Army.... We will prove that the Rosenbergs stole, through David Greenglass, the one weapon *that might well hold the key to the survival of this nation, and means the peace of the world—the atomic bomb!*

The evidence, at least the evidence presented in *Inquest*, does anything but.

Twenty-nine-year-old David Greenglass is called to the stand. Meanwhile, the various "reconstructions" begin to intercut with the courtroom action: Julius and Ethel being questioned by the FBI, a flashback to 1938 and the Rosenbergs' courtship (which, Freed notes, begins "the personal time chamber of Ethel and Julius Rosenberg"). It is a sort of "at-home-with-the-Rosenbergs"—sentimental little vignettes of their marriage and of family relationships, scenes in which Julius delights in a Brooklyn Dodger baseball victory and Ethel in the folk singing of Josh White and, yes, even one little family squabble, presumably intended to show they were human after all. Human, of course, is exactly the thing they seem not to be. Could they really never have talked about anything remotely connected with what was going on around them? Were they so completely "good," so saintlike, that they were impervious to the hysteria of the times and the drama they were caught up in? Were they really *that* one-dimensional?

All the while, David Greenglass's testimony continues. He tells of how Julius told Greenglass's wife, Ruth, "that I was working on the atomic bomb project at Los Alamos and that they would want me to give information to the Russians," and how, in January, 1945, he gave Julius "the information he wanted....It included sketches on the lens molds and how they were used in experiments." Amid the anti-Communist hysteria of the period, the rudimentary nature of these and subsequent sketches, much remarked upon ever since, seems to have been almost totally ignored. David then tells of the celebrated Jello-box side which, when the two cut pieces were matched, would enable the Greenglasses to identify whoever came to them to collect subsequent information, and of how Harry Gold was that contact:

THE GOVERNMENT: Did you tell him what you had for him?

DAVID GREENGLASS: Yes. And I told him, "I think I have a pretty good—a pretty good description of the atom bomb."

THE GOVERNMENT: The atom bomb itself?

DAVID GREENGLASS: That's right.

And so the testimony proceeds. David recalls a watch allegedly given to Julius "as a reward" by the Russians and a console table Julius showed him that "could be used for photograph purposes."

Smirking, self-satisfied, resentful, David Greenglass was of course a quite unlovely figure, as was the prosecution's other major witness, Harry Gold. The former was perhaps a pathological liar, almost certainly a man inclined to fantasy and demonstrations of self-importance. Gold, the Philadelphia chemist and self-confessed Soviet courier who supplied much of the "evidence" in the case after his own conviction and sentencing, is less explicable. The passage of time has certainly rendered much of his testimony suspect. There was, of course, additional evidence—some three dozen prosecution exhibits—convoluted, inconsistent, and sometimes contradictory, and additional testimony, but Greenglass and Gold provided the heart of the government's case. Without them, there could not have been a "Rosenberg trial."

31

It is now generally conceded that the defense was, as Walter Goodman put it in *The New York Times Magazine*, "remarkably inept." Rather than refuting the testimony—something that was perhaps impossible in view of its heavy reliance on the oral—Bloch attacked the witnesses as liars, crooks, and madmen. Freed never really hints at this failure. At the time, most Americans were left with the feeling that the Rosenbergs indeed may have—or indeed *did*, depending on the credibility attributed to Greenglass and Gold—seek the secrets they were alleged to have turned over to the Russians. But, as Goodman has noted, "that they had in fact secured such secrets from the likes of David Greenglass was a matter of some conjecture."

And that is the real problem of *Inquest*. It leaves nothing open to conjecture, permits no areas of gray. Whether the Rosenbergs were in fact guilty "beyond a reasonable doubt" of "conspiracy to commit espionage" and of transmitting atomic bomb secrets to the Russians is the last question it explores. It does not even really ask it. They are presumed innocent—as they unquestionably should have been at the time of the actual trial, but very likely were not—and the remainder of the play is given over to proving (1) what a devoted, bewildered, gallant, lost, lovable and, of course, *100 percent* innocent couple they were: helpless lambs led to the slaughter, and (2) how ruthless, diabolical, anti-Semitic, villainous and, of course, *100 percent* evilly motivated were their persecutors. Not a moment of uncertainty is entertained; not a shred of credible evidence is admitted. The judge is biased to a point that makes even Julius Hoffman, of Chicago Seven fame, seem a paragon of all the juridical virtues.

Admittedly, in rereading some of Judge Irving R. Kaufman's rhetorical pronouncements about "this diabolical conspiracy to destroy a God-fearing nation," it is almost impossible not to conclude that he indeed was caught up in the climate of the time. It is, however, straining credulity to suggest that from top to bottom, from supercilious judge to snarling prosecutors to conniving FBI men, not one court or prosecution figure had a moment without figurative horns and forked tail.

In such a context, even the Rosenbergs' own testimony and their cross-examination lose virtually all ability to convince one

32

of their innocence. It is a world made up exclusively of good guys and bad guys, one in which the exclusion of anything that might raise a doubt ensures the absence of conflict. The audience is asked to decide between two characters who, in their total embodiment of the victim-figure, defy belief, and witnesses who, in appearance, bearing, and assertions seem figures out of one of those Grade-B movies of the 40s, replete with rodentlike informers, bribes, payoffs, and double crosses. One of the reconstructions suggests the attitude:

DAVID GREENGLASS: Julie, I'm in a terrible jam.

JULIUS ROSENBERG: No—I realize you've been asking for money...you've been talking about Mexico. What is the trouble, Dave?

DAVID GREENGLASS: I can't tell you everything about it. All I want you to do for me, Julie, is I gotta have a couple of thousand dollars in cash....

JULIUS ROSENBERG: Dave. I cannot do that.

DAVID GREENGLASS: Julie, I just got to have that money and if you don't get me that money you are going to be sorry.

JULIUS ROSENBERG: Look here, Dave, are you trying to threaten me or blackmail—

DAVID GREENGLASS: I'm warning you.

The difficulty with all this—and with the exhaustively researched 1965 book *Invitation to an Inquest* by Walter and Miriam Schneir on which the play is largely based—is that its acceptance entails granting not only the idea that the Rosenbergs were innocent of any crime whatever—that no crime had in fact been committed—but that the entire case was a frame-up, the prosecution's exhibits were fraudulent, and every witness against the Rosenbergs (not merely those Freed presents) lied at the instigation of the FBI. Freed makes the further mistake of almost entirely ignoring the new evidence the Schneirs and others uncovered in favor of concentrating on the depiction of diabolic monsters out to get what the Rosenberg defense committee often termed "ordinary folks like the vast majority of us."

In his melodramatic-to-maudlin "reconstructions" Freed repeatedly falls back on such bathos as:

> We should tell them what it was like to be poor in New York; a poor Jew, when you two were growing up. *There are no Jews on this jury!* In the meantime, there's three million Jews in this town, but we can't get a Jew on the jury.

I admit to considering this a specious argument, one directly geared to appeal to the Broadway audience, which is predominantly Jewish. Reality demands that Freed and critics dealing with the play recognize that the prosecutor and his associate, Roy M. Cohn, and most of the witnesses were Jewish. Turning the trial into a pogrom will not do.

After the sentencing, one of the panels carries a letter written in childish scrawl and the voice of the Rosenbergs' eight-year-old son, Michael, plaintively begs:

> Dear President Eisenhower: My mommy and daddy are in prison in New York. My brother is six years old, his name is Robbie. Please let my mommy and daddy go and not let anything happen to them. If they come, Robbie and I will be very happy. We will thank you very much.

It just won't work—not as polemic and not as theatre. Freed is simply too disingenuous for plausibility. There are too many cheap demands on the emotions and too few efforts to deal with the trial, its antecedents, and its doubts. As Goodman noted, "given the evidence, the jury's verdict was well within the bounds of reason." Indeed, the defense counsel, Emanuel Bloch, went so far as to compliment the court on the manner in which the trial was conducted. To deny *any* area of doubt, as Freed does, is not just simplistic politically, it is unconvincing theatrically.

34

The handling of the post-trial scenes, which alternate between "reconstructions" based primarily upon the correspond-
ence between the Rosenbergs and their attorney while they
were in prison and courtroom scenes reflecting the various
appeals, only compounds the matter. Ethel sings "Un bel dì,
vedremo" and the "Battle Hymn of the Republic" in her cell
and Julius is told by one of the guards that he's "pretty damn
lucky. Because of her." They talk to each other through a
screen about the visit of their children and Ethel tells her
psychiatrist about her dreams and her fears. Finally, what Freed
calls "the Slow Ritual of Death" begins. As a government
marshal lurks nearby with an open direct-line to Washington in
case they decide to confess and thereby save their lives, they are
led toward the electric chair by a rabbi. It is June 18, 1953,
their fourteenth wedding anniversary. In an excerpt from the
Rosenbergs' final appeal to President Eisenhower for clemency,
they say:

> The guilt in this case, if we die, will be America's. The
> shame, if we die, will dishonor this generation, and
> pervade history until future Americans recapture the
> heritage of truth, justice and equality before the law.

And they die, still denying their involvement or guilt.

With the wisdom of hindsight, it is clear that the degree, not
to mention the certainty, of the Rosenbergs' guilt was at best in
question. It is equally clear that a judge who could become so
caught up in the hysteria and hyperbole of the moment as to
say "Your spying has already caused . . . the Communist aggression in Korea, with the resultant casualties exceeding fifty
thousand and who knows but that millions more of innocent
people must pay the price of your treason" was ill-equipped to
apply the degree of impartiality required in any case, let alone a
capital case. As the French scientist Jacques Monod wrote in a
letter to the *Bulletin of the Atomic Scientists*, much of the
world had "hoped to find that the most powerful nation of the
free world could afford to be at once objective, just, and
merciful."

Today, many things about the trial seem almost unreal and

the execution of the Rosenbergs, whether guilty or innocent, seems a gratuitous, perhaps an unconscionable act. For many outside the U.S. it cast a severe shadow over America's claims to either moral or political leadership at a time long prior to Vietnam. But it did not require Freed's heavy-handed emotionalism and deck-stacking to tell us that. If he ignored substantial evidence and testimony on the part of the prosecution, he ignored additional defense claims as well. The result was a monochromatic play on the sympathies that does precisely what Emanuel Bloch begged the jury not to do: "We come to you and say to you, don't be swayed by emotion. The defendants do not expect you to give a verdict on the basis of sympathy or passion or prejudice. We want you to use your mind and your reason."

Freed precludes the audience from doing either. In denying "at least some element of uncertainty," the defense plea in one of its twenty-three appeals, he ignores his own contention that "the spectator must be given a choice." Without this opportunity to choose there can be no dramatic conflict, no persuasive play, only an ineffectual polemic that speaks exclusively to the converted and has nothing new to say to them. There is a play to be written about the Rosenbergs—and about Sobell—but *Inquest* at no time approaches being that play.

There are people who are willing to protect freedom until there is nothing left of it.

In the Matter of J. Robert Oppenheimer

For a theatre that prides itself on its ability to deal with controversial subject matter, with "breakthroughs," ours has been strangely reluctant to deal with purely political controversy. Despite occasional exceptions in fictionalized form, such as Joseph Heller's *We Bombed in New Haven*, Megan Terry's *Viet Rock*, and David Rabe's *The Basic Training of Pavlo Hummel*, American playwrights seem curiously content to leave the exploration of even our home-grown political dilemmas to the Europeans. There have been exceptions, of course—with Vietnam itself perhaps the liberating exception. It has been partly a question of box office, of course, but somehow it goes considerably beyond that to mirror the fact that effective dramatization of contemporary history and political controversy is largely outside America's admittedly limited theatrical traditions.

For that reason, almost as much as for its intrinsic interest, the production of Heinar Kipphardt's *In the Matter of J. Robert Oppenheimer* was easily one of the most significant American theatrical events of the late 60s, even if it did again require a European to confront us with ourselves, to remind us that there is considerable validity in Kipphardt's contention that "If our theatre is not able to deal with the key political questions of our time, then one will be no longer able to take it seriously.

37

Then it will sink to the level of other media for the manipulation of false sentiments."

In the Matter of J. Robert Oppenheimer was first presented in October, 1964, at the West Berlin Free People's Theatre, and subsequently in France, Italy, and England. Its American premiere did not take place until June, 1968, at the Mark Taper Forum in Los Angeles. Its production almost one year later by the Repertory Theatre of Lincoln Center was one of the major critical and audience successes of the New York season.

Silesia-born Heinar Kipphardt was studying medicine when he was drafted into the German army. He served with a panzer division on the Russian front and deserted in 1944, resuming his medical studies after the war. He has been active in the theatre since 1951, first as a producer at the Deutsches Theatre in Berlin. After nine years, he left East Berlin, settling first in Düsseldorf, then in Munich.

Even allowing for the universal nature of the questions *Oppenheimer* raises, it at first seems odd that it would have been written by a German rather than an American. According to Kipphardt, the play is largely based on the 3,000-page transcript of the hearing held before the Personnel Security Board of the Atomic Energy Commission in April-May, 1954, to rule on Dr. Oppenheimer's security clearance. He decided to write it because he "had firsthand knowledge of where terrible intolerance can lead."

Although some elements in the play are fictionalized, some characters who did not actually appear at the hearing are brought on to testify, and yet other characters are given fictitious names—although, in fact, substantial liberty is taken with the attribution of statements—a large part of the dialog has been taken more or less verbatim from the transcript. "It was impossible to achieve the required concentration with a verbatim reproduction of statement and counterstatement," Kipphardt explains in the published version, "nor did this seem desirable to the author in the interests of the unity of the play. Therefore I endeavored to subordinate word-for-word recapitulation to accuracy of meaning."

Without leaving any doubt where he stands, Kipphardt has maintained substantial if selective fidelity to the truth and the ideological substance of the proceedings. Such things as news-reel clips of the first atomic bomb test explosion, the devastation of Hiroshima, President Truman addressing the American people, and the first hydrogen bomb test, sound track excerpts, and related newspaper headlines are used to ensure that the audience will not become so absorbed in the human drama that it loses track of the fact that, dramatic license aside, what they are watching did happen here, that it in some ways continues to happen.

Despite moments when the interest slackens under the sheer weight of the information being presented, it is an arresting and at times quite powerful piece of theatre. The questions it raises cannot be ignored. Is a man to be punished—or at least denigrated—because his ideas or convictions are unorthodox or unpopular? For his naivete? For his associations of twelve years earlier? Is judgment to be passed on the actions of the past in the light of the greatly changed climate of the present? Where does a man's loyalty belong when there is a seeming conflict between his duty to a state and what he sees as his duty to man-kind? Have scientists abdicated their responsibility when they turn over weapons of mass destruction with the Eichmann-like attitude that what is done with them is not their decision, that they were little more than cogs in a wheel, men following orders for whose consequences they are not accountable? "The drop-ping of the atom bomb on Hiroshima was a political decision—it wasn't mine," Oppenheimer insists at one point, a curious asser-tion for a man who was later to insist on the prerogatives of conscience. He is reminded of the apparent contradiction by the AEC counsel:

ROBB: Did you have moral scruples about how many were killed?

OPPENHEIMER: Terrible ones.

ROBB: You had terrible moral scruples?

OPPENHEIMER: I don't know anyone who would *not* have had terrible moral scruples after the dropping of the bomb.

ROBB: Isn't that a trifle schizophrenic? . . . To produce the thing, to pick the targets, to determine the height at which the explosion has the maximum effect—and then to be overcome by moral scruples at the consequences. . . .

OPPENHEIMER: Yes. . . . It is the kind of schizophrenia we physicists have been living with for several years now.

In another sense, however, the essential question raised by *Oppenheimer* is whether we may, in protecting freedom, protect freedom out of existence. It was the question referred to by Lincoln when he asked, "Must a government of necessity be too strong for the liberties of its people or too weak to maintain its own existence?" And, of course, it was the question alluded to by the actual board that investigated Oppenheimer, when it acknowledged, "We are acutely aware that in a very real sense this case puts the security system of the United States on trial."

These and many similar issues arise as the AEC panel meets in Room 2022 in Building T3 of the Atomic Energy Commission in Washington to question Oppenheimer "concerning his views, his associations, his actions, suspected of disloyalty." In the end, however, the issues are narrowed down primarily to two: his earlier association with Communists and Communist sympathizers, especially his friendship with Haakon Chevalier, whom he shielded from suspicion of espionage, and his opposition to the development of the hydrogen bomb, an opposition that allegedly resulted in a substantial delay in its production.

The panel calls its witnesses: Oppenheimer's fellow scientists—Edward Teller, Hans Bethe, I. I. Rabi (the latter called "Jacob Lehmann" in the production, though not in the published text)—security officers, and an Air Force technical adviser. Friends and adversaries, those who envy and those who admire, those merely doing what they see as their job, alternately defend and indict him. It is, however, the time of McCarthy and, as one witness remarks, "lawful criteria are being obliterated by fear and demagoguery." In such an atmosphere, the events of the 30s, the fact that Oppenheimer's wife, brother, and several of his friends and colleagues had at one time or another been Communists and that he himself acknowledged having been a fellow-traveler many years earlier is considered damning, retrospective guilt, guilt by association. It is ignored that

> what so many people are doing today, is looking at events which took place in 1941, 1942, and judging them in the light of their present feelings. But human behavior varies in the changing context of time. If associations in the thirties or forties are regarded in the same light as similar associations would be regarded today—then, in my view, it is a manifestation of the current hysteria.

In many ways, Oppenheimer was his own worst witness, a curious blend of arrogance and naivete, who insisted on what he, at least, viewed as logic, a man committed to the power of argument in a time when the nation that surrounded him was committed to the power of emotion. In such a context, the outcome is seldom in doubt—and even less frequently vindicated by history. The idea that Oppenheimer's then heretical opinions concerning the necessity for arms control and the dangers of a too exclusive reliance on the so-called superweapons eventually would be proclaimed national policy must at the time have seemed farfetched indeed. Today, it is but one of many ironies.

In one of the key exchanges of the play, Gordon Gray, who chaired the security board, questions Oppenheimer regarding his opposition to initiating a crash program to develop the hydrogen bomb at the time when he was chairman of the General Advisory Committee of the AEC:

> GRAY: Would you not say, Dr. Oppenheimer, that such an attitude might imply something like divided loyalty?
>
> OPPENHEIMER: Divided between whom?
>
> GRAY: Loyalty to a government—loyalty to mankind. . . .
>
> OPPENHEIMER: I would like to put it this way: if

41

governments show themselves unequal to, or not sufficiently equal to, the new scientific discoveries— then the scientist *is* faced with these conflicting loyalties. . . .

GRAY: You do not want to say that it is right to give one's undivided loyalty to the government in every case?

OPPENHEIMER: I don't know. I think about it. But I have always done it.

In a sense, much of the testimony at the hearing constituted something of a chimera, cloaking as it did the sort of interdepartmental disputes and personal rivalries that remain very much a part of life in Washington. In the case of Oppenheimer, the Strategic Air Command had come to resent both the fact that his advice on policy, particularly in such areas as nuclear-powered aircraft (where the validity of his doubts was to be confirmed), often was in conflict with SAC goals, and his immense prestige and influence. Perhaps wisely (in theatrical terms), Kipphardt does not really explore the ramifications of such rivalries. For the historian—indeed, for anyone who seeks to understand fully what took place in that hearing room in 1954—they remain, part shadow, part substance, of the reasons underlying the eventual findings.

By the time the hearing was completed after more than three weeks of testimony, the commission had heard some forty witnesses. The report it returned was perhaps even more schizophrenic than the schizophrenia of Oppenheimer's own earlier attitude and behavior:

Although we have no doubt that he gave his advice with loyal intent and to the best of his ability, we note a deplorable lack of faith in the United States government, a lack of faith which is exemplified by his endeavor to prevent the development of the hydrogen bomb by means of international agreements, and is further exemplified by his demand for a guarantee that we shall not be the first to use that weapon. We find that his conduct gives rise to considerable doubt as to whether his future participation in a national defense program would be unequivocally compatible with the requirements of the country's security. . . . We conclude that Dr. Oppenheimer can no longer claim the unreserved confidence of the government and of the Atomic Energy Commission.

The questions raised by *In the Matter of J. Robert Oppenheimer* are as pertinent today as they were at the height of the McCarthy period. The equation of dissent with disloyalty and the struggle for supremacy between the civilian and the military go on, albeit with somewhat greater finesse on most occasions. The rules of the game have not really changed. "We should have knocked before opening the door to the horrible world in which we now live," Oppenheimer observes at one point. "But we preferred to break the door down. Although it gave us no strategic advantage." It is one of the many ironies of Kipphardt's play, and of Oppenheimer's life, that as the New York premiere at the Repertory Theatre of Lincoln Center explored the matter of J. Robert Oppenheimer by night, the U.S. Congress was exploring the question of the ABM by day. It was difficult not to hear the echoes. Echoes continue to surround us.

We walkin' around practically
worshippin' death. We so eager
to die that we forgot how to
live. The revolution gonna fail
if we keep this up. . . . We got
to offer our people life, y'all.
Not more death.

The Black Terror

Late in Richard Wesley's *The Black Terror* a member of the
guerrilla Black Terrorist Organization challenges his leader:
"But suppose the people don't want a revolution?" It's a
question you somehow don't expect to hear these days, at least
not in a play written by a twenty-seven-year-old black writer,
writing for an all-black cast. But, then, there are many surprising things—for blacks or whites—in Wesley's powerful and
unstereotyped play.

The Black Terror is set in what is described as "the very near
future, given the nature of American society." Its principal
character, Keusi Kifo ("Black Death"), is in his mid-twenties
and has recently returned from Vietnam. While there, he has
become a proficient killer, a marksman to be reckoned with.
Now, still an initiate in the organization, he is assigned the
mission of assassinating the police commissioner:

> You kneel before me having been chosen by vote to
> carry out a mission of assassination against the most
> vicious and ruthless enemy of the people in this area.

45

Your target is Police Commissioner Charles Savage, organizer of the mad-dog Night Rangers of the police department. He is an avowed enemy of the revolution and he is therefore an Oppressor. He must die.

Although Keusi has doubts about murder as a revolutionary weapon (he knows the price of war and killing), he agrees. A young girl named M'Bahlia, who has broken away from her middle-class black background to become "an outstanding revolutionary and an expert terrorist," becomes his partner, joined with him until the mission is carried out or terminated by Antar, the terrorists' leader. In addition to helping Keusi prepare for his task, she will do for him "all those things a man expects of a woman," acting as his "wife" until the mission is completed.

They live together in a tenement apartment and, predictably, they fall in love. At least Keusi falls in love; M'Bahlia is more resistant. She is also resistant to his desire to find a relatively safe way to carry out the assassination, a way that will give him more chance of escaping than the highway ambush the organization has proposed:

I don't accept the inevitability of a revolutionary death. Understand? He who assassinates and gets away shall live to assassinate another day—if he's clever. And I intend to be clever. I ain't hardly suicidal.

Which, at the very least, would seem to distinguish Keusi from his brother plotters.

M'Bahlia rejects his feelings of compassion for the man he is about to kill. Charles Savage is the Oppressor, the enemy, the devil, the beast. He is "a non-man . . . a no thing. . . . Compassion is beyond the emotional range of the true terrorist." Revolutionary fervor is the only true emotion in the revolution, she insists, and, she says, "I'm a revolutionary before I'm a woman."

Before he can kill Savage, the Night Rangers raid the head-

46

quarters of the American Liberation Front and twenty-two people, among them thirteen policemen, are killed. Geronimo, the wounded leader of the ALF, is brought to the Black Terrorist headquarters. Three of his best men have been killed; others are wounded or in hiding; the records are probably in police hands. Because of it, the whole ALF must go underground. A little foresight on Geronimo's part might have averted it—both the deaths and the debacle. The Black Terrorists sense this, but Geronimo is a dedicated brother, a courageous revolutionary. They can only concur when he shouts:

> Death and destruction! Pain and agony! Let the blood of the enemy flow in the streets purifying the revolutionary cause. Let nothing remain standing before the power of the revolution!!!

Keusi feels differently, not only about the effectiveness of wholesale killing but about the effectiveness of Geronimo's leadership. Why, he demands of M'Bahlia, did Geronimo pursue the battle with the police, with the result that nine of his organization died and their headquarters burned? "His back wasn't totally to the wall. . . . I know that the gunfight wasn't necessary." M'Bahlia is outraged, and even more so when he laughs at her insistence she is "a revolutionary—a Black Terrorist. Sex isn't a thing with me anymore. . . . A true revolutionary has no time for such emotions." But her reluctance is relatively short-lived and, after Keusi successfully fulfills his mission the next day, using not a gun but a crossbow, she begins to be more responsive to his somewhat unrevolutionary ardor.

The completion of his mission has made Keusi something of a hero even among the Black Terrorists who earlier questioned his lack of commitment to violence. Even so, his moment in the revolutionary sun is a brief one. When he next goes to the headquarters and is given his new assignment—the assassination of Chauncey Radcliffe, a black moderate who has turned in three of the Terrorists' men to the police and sworn to destroy the black militants, whom he holds responsible for the death of his son—Keusi at first balks at the idea of killing another black, then reluctantly agrees. He does have reservations:

47

> Once you get a rep for killing your own people,
> popular support starts to dwindle. . . . Who are we to
> decide what Black people will die? We got no man-
> date from the people.

It is really only now that Wesley is getting to the core of the
question *The Black Terror* raises: the efficacy of violence, and,
more particularly, killing, as a weapon in the revolution. Unlike
most of those who have dealt with this theme, he refuses to
come down hard on one side or the other. At the present
moment in the struggle, there is something to be said for both,
and Wesley is determined that it will be said. Because Keusi is
the more articulate, because he has history on his side and his
principal antagonist, Geronimo, has only passion, the more
moderate viewpoint is at least intellectually more convincing.

Keusi insists that the murder of Radcliffe will be only the
beginning, that preachers will be next "'cause a lotta them
shuckin' and jivin', too." After that will come teachers, who
after all work in the Oppressor's schools, and black government
officials, and . . . Where *will* the line be drawn?

ANTAR: We always deal with the wishes of the people.
The people wished the Oppressor Savage dead and we
fulfilled that wish. Deep down they want Radcliffe
dead. We will fulfill that wish, too.

KEUSI: But suppose the people don't want a revolution? Suppose they ain't really ready?

AHMED: That's what we mean when we say that the
people don't always know what's good for them.

KEUSI: But if we represent the people, we gotta always
be responsible to them. . . . We should never try to
operate independent from the people. I don't know,
man, but somewhere along the line I think we got a
fucked-up set of values. . . . Can't no revolution be
successfully carried out without the support of the
people. . . . And when you get into offin' Black
people as though you were some omnipotent agents

48

from heaven or someplace then, hey, man, you sealin'
your own doom.

In response, Geronimo has only more revolutionary rhetoric
to offer, more talk of the "revolutionary vanguard," more talk
of the Oppressors dying and blood flowing. "Is that all you got
to offer the people, man? Death?" Keusi asks. "Why not wage a
revolution directed toward life?"

Geronimo and Keusi battle verbally. Keusi blames him for
the fact that those killed in the raid died needlessly and because
Geronimo did not keep his cool and use the escape tunnel
earlier. But, no, Geronimo contends, they weren't cowards;
they weren't going to run.

GERONIMO: I'm a revolutionary. My job is to kill the
enemy, foment revolution among the people, and lay
my life on the line if necessary, for the revolution.

KEUSI: You not a revolutionary. You an angry Brother
with a gun. You filled your head fulla a whole lotta
slogans and you followin' an ideal that somebody
lifted from the fucked-up minds of some nihilistic
white boys who lived a hundred years ago.

Geronimo loses his cool completely and pulls a gun on Keusi,
accusing him of standing in the way of the revolution, of
destroying their beliefs. Just as he is about to fire, Antar hits his
arm and the pistol misfires. After Geronimo is helped to his
quarters, Antar asserts that, although some of his points may
have been valid, Keusi has behaved in an undisciplined and
counterrevolutionary manner and is being suspended from all
revolutionary activities other than indoctrination classes.

But Keusi will have no more of it. "Maybe I'll just go into the
Black community and educate the kids as to what I have
learned in the world," he tells M'Bahlia. "Maybe that's the only
thing I can do. But I can't stay here."

M'Bahlia refuses to go with him; she has sworn her life to the
revolution. Keusi tries in vain to convince her she is wrong:

When the revolution really begins and homes and
neighborhoods get burned down, and blood really

49

flows in the streets, and we face the full-scale cracker
retaliation, you'll see what I was talkin' about. You'll
see how far blind revolutionary zeal will get Black
people living in White America. . . . This ain't Asia,
baby. We ain't got an endless supply of manpower.

M'Bahlia is forced to admit that his arguments are
persuasive—but not persuasive enough. If oppression is to end,
they *must* fight. Otherwise, yet more generations of black
people will be born to live under it. "We must have our manhood and womanhood and we must have it now, or America
will simply have to die."

In the meantime, she tells him to go: she must prepare for a
mission, one that will provide her with "the ultimate freedom a
true revolutionary can have." She is to kill Radcliffe. "The
revolution takes precedence over everything."

Just what "everything" may mean becomes clear when
M'Bahlia appears at Radcliffe's home. Chauncey Radcliffe is her
father. His intentions have been good. Or have they simply been
misguided, as she tells him? He insists that he understands her
frustration and her bitterness. He must, however, fight against
her revolution because he doesn't want to see more black
women "crying over the bodies of their Black men," or more of
them die "needlessly and senselessly against hopeless odds." He
pleads with her "to give up this madness and come back home."
It is to no avail.

M'BAHLIA: If it's madness we're into then it's madness
that will change this world! . . . I'll never be free until
I'm free of this oppression that I have had to deal
with all my life. And most of all, as a revolutionary, I
can never be free until I'm free of you.

A moment later, she pulls a gun and shoots him in the head.

As *The Black Terror* ends, the voice of a radio newscaster is
heard. Acting on information received from Radcliffe, the
police have raided the headquarters of the Black Terrorists.
Scores lie dying—men, women, and children, police and revolutionaries. An on-the-spot reporter says:

50

The police rampaged through the halls like madmen.... They were like, like savages. I couldn't believe it. These men are good Americans. What went wrong?! What went wrong?! ... So far, I have seen not one Black alive. The police are killing them all. They're just shooting. It's unbelievable! I keep saying to myself, "This is America. It can't be happening! Not in America!" ... The Blacks are fighting like crazed animals.... I don't understand all this. Why are they fighting so hard?! What can America have done to them that would make them resort to this insanity?

At the end, Antar, Ahmed, and M'Bahlia are holding out at the top of the stairs, perhaps the only ones left. And, still, the white reporter asks: "Why do they fight so hard?! ... We'll give them a chance if they would only act like Americans."

And the play ends: with dynamite exploding amid the gunshots, screams, and shouts; with a spot on the Specter of Death, draped in an American flag, clenched fist upraised.

Who has been right? Keusi, with his belief that the revolution must offer its people "life and not more death," that in the face of vastly superior numbers and resources it is folly to take on the Man in an area where he cannot be defeated? Or the Black Terrorists, convinced that death is preferable to submission and killing a revolutionary virtue? Wesley makes the case for both, and with surprising balance and even objectivity. He has little patience with revolutionary rhetoric when it flies in the face of revolutionary reality.

But the play is anything but an intellectual exercise. It resounds with the passion and intensity of a writer committed to the need for answers in an area where he knows "answers" may not exist. Wesley does tend to overwrite, to permit his characters to repeat their points long after those points have been scored, and, especially in the early stages, the repeated anti-Oppressor clichés and jargon become somewhat wearing. But these are relatively minor flaws in a work that is more multifaceted, more nuanced, in its presentation of the varying viewpoints on violence within the black community than several

51

that have been far more celebrated. Wesley refuses to simplify, and in so doing he probes not merely the problem but the hearts and minds of his audience, whether black or white.

We was got the day we was born! Where you been? Jus' bein' black ain't never been no real reason for livin'.

No Place to Be Somebody

Johnny's Bar. It is in Greenwich Village, and it is in Gabe Gabriel's head—perhaps more in Gabe's head. He is an actor and a writer—an actor whose "black" skin is so light he cannot get a role as a black, a writer who tells you in the opening speech that he is working on a play and that he is "gonna make it all up in my head as I go along." But, he warns the audience, it isn't "a figment of my grassy imagination." It is real, as real as his pain, as real as the torment, the pain, and the anguish of nearly all the characters in Charles Gordone's powerful and lacerating "Black-black comedy" *No Place to Be Somebody.*

Shanty Mulligan is the first we meet. He is a young white man, a junkie and a handyman of sorts in Johnny's Bar. White, but wanting desperately to be black. With his ever-present drumsticks, rapping rhythmically on bar and table top, he lives off his myth of the past—his one great jam session when he sat in for Max Roach and "Ol Red Taylor said wasn't nobody could hold a beat an' steady cook it like me. Said I had 'the thing'!" Shanty is going to get himself another set of drums; he is going to make his "comeback"—someday.

Then there is Johnny Williams himself: young, angry, and black. He runs his bar, but runs it at the sufferance of Pete Zerroni and his white Mafia-style henchmen. "Crackers cain't

53

'magine Niggers runnin' nothin' but elevators an' toilets," he tells Shanty. And Johnny knows; he has tried often enough to be a *black* operator. From the time when he was a kid, an orphan who benefited from the tutelage of Sweets Crane, who treated him "like his own son," he has meant to be somebody. Sweets has taught him how to play the white man's game, if not how to beat him at it. Johnny intends to figure out that final step. He has a scheme and, he says to Gabe, "the scheme is together." Sweets is about to get out of prison after a ten-year stretch and "me an' him gon' git us a piece'a this town."

Gabe will have no part of it. He isn't looking to break the law. Johnny is scornful:

> They ain't no law. They kill you an' me in the name'a the law. You an' me wouldn't be where we at, if it wasn't for the law. Even the laws they write for us makes us worse off.

Gabe's hatred is of another kind. He has spent his life working at not losing his temper. His mind is the vessel for his rage, but that rage is going to remain closely contained. It is only in his head—only to the audience—that he admits what is going on, how "deep down inside things begin to happen"; how he sometimes gets "so vicious, I wanna go out an' commit mass murder." But, just as quickly, he insists he's not "hung up on crap like persecution an' hatred."

Although Gabe calls himself a black playwright, he is going to leave "that violence jazz" to those who are better at it. But, in his head and in Johnny's Bar, there is "that violence jazz" and, even more, his recollections of how "those dirty-black people" moved out of "that dirty-black slum" to a "clean-white neighborhood" and "grew up clean and keen" only to find that no matter "how hard we scrubbed, it was only making us blacker!" Blacker and more the victims of hypocrisy. In one of the prologues with which Gabe opens each act, he observes:

> Yes! They's mo' to bein' black than meets
> The eye!
> Bein' black has a way'a makin' ya mad mos'

54

Of the time, hurt all the time an' havin'
So many hangups, the problem'a soo-side
Don't even enter yo' min'! It's buyin'
What you don't want, beggin' what you don't
Need! An' stealin' what is yo's by rights! Yes!
They's mo' to bein' black than meets the
Eye!

Meanwhile, the frequenters of Johnny's Bar come and go: black and white whores, one of whom Johnny pimps for; a black practical nurse named Cora, who is in love with Shanty and promises to help him get a new set of drums; a short-order cook named Melvin, who is studying dancing; and a new face, Mary Lou Bolton, a white girl, just out of college and ready to lecture Johnny on how she is involved in picketing a nearby construction site because "the unions won't accept qualified Negroes." Why, Johnny challenges, don't those qualified Negroes "do they own pickitin'?" Mary Lou goes off to carry her civil rights placard. She will, however, be back.

Finally, Sweets Crane arrives. But he is not the Sweets Johnny remembers; he is not the dude with three hundred suits who was "into some'a ev'thing." He is obviously ill—dying, as it turns out—and he has had his fill of the action. Johnny doesn't believe it. But Johnny has the "Charlie fever." Sweets tells him:

I gave it to you.... Way we was raised, husslin' an' usin' yo' biscuit to pull quickies was the only way we could feel like we was men. Couldn't copy Charlie's good points an' live like men. So we copied his bad points.... We just pissed away our lives tryin' to be bad like Charlie.... All it did was make us hate him all the more an' ourselves too. Then I tried to go horse-to-horse with 'em up there in the Bronx. An' ended up with a ten.... Seems to me, the worse sickness'a man kin have is the Charlie fever.

And Johnny Williams has a bad case of it. He, too, wants to go "horse-to-horse" with the white man, to have his black Mafia. That it won't be well received by Pete Zerroni is clear

55

two days later when one of his "community relations" men shows up in the bar to warn Johnny not to have anything to do with any plans Sweets may have. Sweets, however, has no plans. He is dying and in his will he has left Johnny an interest in various stores and real estate that he has accumulated over the years.

It obviously isn't going to work out that way. Johnny has no desire to go straight, to give up his plan. As he starts to pursue it, it becomes evident that quite a few may get hurt along the way. One of the first is Dee, his white whore, whom he is ready to cast aside in favor of Mary Lou. Mary Lou, it seems, is the daughter of a judge, and that judge was the lawyer for Pete Zerroni at a time when he was on trial for murder and attempting to bribe a city official. Dee has realized that Johnny is involved with another woman. As she sits in the bar drinking in his absence, she gets drunker by the minute. Finally, she opens her purse, removes a can of black shoe polish, and starts to apply it to her face. Just at that moment, Johnny comes in. When Mary Lou arrives seconds later, Dee runs off, drunkenly telling Johnny to "run away from here fast. Run for your life." But it is not her life Dee runs for; it is toward her death. She slashes her wrists in the ladies' room of the Hotel Theresa.

No Place to Be Somebody is a play of dying dreams. It is not only that Dee fails to get out of "the life" and to marry Johnny. There is Shanty. When Cora buys him his drums, the drums he has so boasted of playing and has so yearned to have replaced, they come back with them to Johnny's. It is to be his moment of triumph, the moment when he can finally show them the truth of his past glories, the moment at which he can quit his job in the bar and move on to claim his future. Shanty sits down at the drums, nervously fumbles with them, taps on the cymbals, then begins. He becomes louder and louder, more and more wild, frantic almost to the point of possession. But there is nothing there. If he ever "played like 'a spade," he can no longer. But he will not, perhaps cannot, stop, until finally Johnny pours a pitcher of water over his head. It is a moment of shame, of anguish, for Cora. Shanty leaps up, shouting, "I had it! I was on it! I was into it, babee!" But Shanty will never be musically black, never have the kind of "soul" he aspires to

56

and claims. So he must turn on Cora, turn on her because by
buying him the drums she has caused him to reveal the hollowness of his claims and of his dreams.

"You don't want me to play no drums," he accuses her.
"Thought you'd make a fool out'a me, did you? Gittin' me to
bring these drums in here. You thought I'd mess it up. Well, I
showed you where it was at. I showed all'a you." He insists that
she call the store to come and get the drums; he does not need
her to buy them for him. He will get his own—someday. Meanwhile, they are through. It is the only way he can hang on to
some fragment of his dream, avoid his humiliation. "What
happens to a dream deferred?" asked Langston Hughes. For
Shanty at least, it does not explode.

Johnny's dreams, too, are doomed, though he does not yet
know it. "Someone" has called Mary Lou's father and told him
to stop her from seeing Johnny. Johnny insists it is because
Zerroni is afraid he may be able to obtain through her some of
her father's records on the Zerroni case and use them to keep
Zerroni off his back. Zerroni "don't like it if a Nigger's got a
place'a business in his ter'tory." Mary Lou tells him there are
people they can go to for help. Johnny demurs:

> You liberal-ass white people kill me! All the time
> know more 'bout wha's bes' for Niggers'n Niggers do.

> MARY LOU: You don't have to make the world any
> worse.

> JOHNNY: Never had no chance to make it no better
> neither.

Mary Lou gets him his records and his tape from her father's
safe. The information he wants about the murder and the bribe
is all there. And it is his undoing, for he has wanted it not, as he
told Mary Lou, to keep Zerroni from forcing him out of business, but in order to blackmail his way into his own racket.
When Gabe tells her, she refuses to believe it, but Johnny
acknowledges, "I gotta right to my own game. Just like they
do."

But not for long. A day later, the judge appears with two
plainclothesmen. Mary Lou has been picked up for trying to

57

solicit an officer and she has claimed she was working for him. Before they take him in, however, the judge is willing to strike a bargain: Johnny's freedom for the notes and tape. Johnny agrees, or seems to; but Johnny has had copies made. The judge is satisfied, but Zerroni's henchman Maffucci, who shows up moments later, is not. Zerroni may be willing to forget it all, but for Maffucci, it doesn't "look good on my record."

Sweets attempts to defend Johnny with a knife and is shot, the first death in a series of almost *Hamlet* proportions, which eventually finds not only Sweets but Maffucci, his partner, and Johnny strewn about the barroom floor. Johnny, however, dies not at Maffucci's hand, but at Gabe's. He has promised Sweets, as he lay dying, that he will go straight, get rid of "the Cholly fever." It is a promise he has no intention of keeping. "It's your war too, Nigger," he tells Gabe. "Why can't you see that? You wanna go on believin' in the lie. We at war, Gabe! Black ag'inst white." He taunts him that he is a "lousy, yellow, screamin' faggot coward." But Johnny has gone too far. Gabe kills him, wipes off the gun, places it in his hand, and then leaves, only to return in a brief and curious epilogue.

He is dressed as a woman in mourning, a spokesman for black anguish:

> I will weep, I will wail, and I will mourn. But my cries will not be heard. No one will wipe away my bitter tears. My black anguish will fall upon deaf ears. I will mourn a passing! Yes. The passing of the ending of a people dying. Of a people dying into that new life. A people whose identity could only be measured by the struggle, the dehumanization, the degradation they suffered. Or allowed themselves to suffer perhaps.

The tone is somehow wrong, false even. It fails to jibe with the harsh and bitter reality and the ironic humor that have gone before. For what has gone before, for all its melodrama and its sometime lack of discipline, has a pungency, an immediacy, and a cohesiveness that that last gesture somehow violates. But it is one of the very few wrong steps. *No Place to Be Somebody* vibrates with a kind of vitality all too seldom found on contemporary stages. It may sprawl; it may on occasion become self-indulgent or sentimental; it never bores. It is alive.

*And then I thought, ah, how
terrible it would be if we
finally owe to the white man
not only our destruction, but
also our glory.*

Indians

Amid stereophonic tom-toms and unidentifiable animal sounds,
Buffalo Bill comes galloping on, astride a specially devised
stage horse; it rears back nervously, shying when the lights
begin to blaze. Strobes flash, loudspeakers scattered about
the theatre remind Bill to get on with the show as he attempts
to elicit the audience's sympathy over the fact that his manager,
"a . . . rather *ancient* gentleman, made a terrible *mistake . . . .*
Well! I dunno what you folks know 'bout show business, but le'
me tell you, there is nothin' more depressin' than playin'
two-a-day in a goddam ghost town!"

It is Buffalo Bill's Wild West Show, an "absolutely original
heroic enterprise of inimitable lustre" (as the posters proclaim),
"the only exhibition in all the world that has no counter-
part . . . exclusively its own creation." At a preview of the New
York production, a boy of ten or eleven in the row ahead of me
leaned forward eagerly; in the next row a gentleman muttered
to his wife, "I hope this isn't a play of 'social relevance.'" I'm
afraid both may have been a trifle disappointed.

Arthur Kopit's *Indians* owes its inspiration to that "social
relevance" and its externals to show biz, and only erratically do
the twain satisfactorily meet. In its third and presumably defini-

tive version (it was presented in somewhat different form in London and Washington) it is an amalgam of bitter truths and broad farce, an *almost* scathing indictment of the hypocrisy of white America and a reluctant, perhaps unconscious, compromise with that America's audiences. Even so, there are moments, regrettably only moments, when it is one helluva piece of theatre.

The New York production and the published version of *Indians* revealed a play that was both better and worse than when it was presented by the Royal Shakespeare Company in London in 1968. Better because its narrative line and central character had been somewhat clarified, worse because its parallels with today had become muted and its humor, broad enough to begin with, had been further coarsened to the point of what, at times, seems calculated crudity. At the same time, the comic-strip quality of much of the RSC production, with its painted faces and Uncle Sam-attired president, was abandoned. In the background, the contemporary parallels with America's exploitation of the Indians—the parallels with white treatment of the blacks and the American role in Vietnam—remained, at least dimly, for those who sought them.

Kopit employs what is, in effect, a dual framework—on the one hand the investigation of Indian grievances by a presidential commission at the Standing Rock reservation, on the other, Buffalo Bill's Wild West Show. The juxtaposition of the Indians' dignity with the white man's farce, of the glory that was the former's heritage and the hypocrisy that is the latter's, is dominant. If he makes *Indians* too much a rerun in reverse of the day when cowboys were automatically the good guys and Indians bloodthirsty savages, Kopit for the most part does avoid the sort of sentimentality his material might have led to.

He does not, however, altogether avoid making his Indians seem just a bit too gullible in their explanations of how it all came about. John Grass tells the commission:

> I am going to talk about what the Great Father told us a long time ago. He told us to give up hunting and start farming. So we did as he said, and our people grew hungry. . . . So the Great Father said he would

62

send us food and clothing, but nothing came of it. So we asked him for the money he had promised us when we sold him the Black Hills, thinking, with this money we could *buy* food and clothing. But nothing came of it. So we grew ill and sad. . . . So we said to the Great Father that we thought we would like to go *back* to hunting, because to live, we needed food. But we found that while we had been learning to farm, the buffalo had gone away. And the plains were filled now only with their bones.

It is, of course, Buffalo Bill, the very man who has brought the commission to listen to the Indians' grievances, who was largely responsible for the fact that "the buffalo had gone away." A series of flashbacks recalls such events as his slaughter of 4,280 buffalo to provide food for the railroad workers going west, the event that earned him the nickname Buffalo Bill. ("It wasn't my fault!" he later insists. "The railroad men needed food. They *hired* me to find 'em food! Well. How was *I* t'know the goddam buffalo reproduced so slowly? *How was I to know that?* NO ONE KNEW THAT!") There is the expedition west in honor of the Russian Grand Duke Alexis, for which Cody served as a guide, which launches him on the telling of ever-taller tales concerning his prowess and bravery, and the embroiderment and defilement of his myth which followed upon the inauguration of his Wild West Show. It is not that he does not have an explanation: "Ya see, Bill," he tells Wild Bill Hickok when they go to perform at the White House, "what you fail to understand is that I'm not being false to what I *was*. I'm simply *drawin'* on what I was . . . and raisin' it to a higher level." Of such self-deceptions and duplicity, Kopit suggests, are our national legends—and our national tragedies—made.

Kopit is concerned with past and present, with the Indians and the blacks we destroyed, and with the Asians we are destroying. It is impossible not to hear the latter-day echoes as he unfolds how Washington reneged on Jefferson's pledge that "not a foot of land will be taken from the Indians without their consent" and upon various treaties as well. If there is a bit too much of the stereotyped noble savage to Kopit's Indians, they are moving nonetheless, especially when given their own words, as with Chief Joseph's speech of surrender. He is reduced to repeating it before Buffalo Bill's Wild West Show audiences: "My heart is sick and sad. From where the sun now stands, I will fight no more forever."

Through it all, Buffalo Bill himself wanders, bemused, blustering, justifying, only half understanding the role he has taken on for both white men and Indians. "I had a dream," he says, "that I was gonna help people, great numbers of people." He is the ineffectual, well-intentioned man with his heart at least partly in the right place, the man whose tragedy is that he knows not what he does, save perhaps at the moment when he realizes that the government has ordered and brought about the death of his friend Sitting Bull, "the greatest Indian who'd ever lived," and massacred most of his tribe. "I'm scared," he tells Hickok. "I dunno what's happenin' anymore. . . . Things have gotten . . . *beyond* me." He sees the fallen Indians everywhere and he is frightened, "not so much of *dyin'*, but . . . dyin' wrong . . . in the center of my arena with . . . makeup on." Somewhere along the line the myth has taken over; he no longer "knows who he *is*."

But even now, as the shadows surround him, he retains something of his ability to deceive himself, something of his ability to rationalize everything to conform with the legend he and the public relations men have propagated. He is echoed by the justifications for the massacre put forth to the press by the army's commanding officer. They are lines that could be—and have been—spoken nearly a century later:

> I don't like it any more than you. But had we shirked our responsibility, skirmishes would have gone on for years, costing our country millions, as well as untold lives. Of course innocent people have been killed. In war they always are. And of course our hearts go out to the innocent victims of this. But war is not a game. . . . In the long run I believe what happened here at this reservation yesterday will be justified.

There are facile reactions on both sides. And there is the

64

spirit of Sitting Bull, the Indian who insisted on the retention of his dignity, on the fact that his people were a great people, reminding Cody, "We had land. . . . You wanted it; you took it. That . . . I understand perfectly. What I cannot understand . . . is why you did all this, *and at the same time* . . . professed your love." A moment later, Sitting Bull states the fact that comes close to the essence of their relationship: "We were on reservations. We could not fight, or hunt. We could do nothing. Then you came and allowed us to imitate our glory. . . . It was humiliating! For sometimes, we could almost imagine it was *real*."

In the end, everyone has been reduced—the exploiters and the exploited—and Buffalo Bill comes forward to the footlights to peddle his phony souvenirs of the civilization that was, the trinkets and the moccasins, the beads and the feathered headdresses, the picture postcards and the Navaho dolls. All to "help them help themselves," for the mockery, the final irony, must be acted out. There must be the "handsome replica of an Indian. Made of genuine wood." Obviously, there must not be the Indian himself, only Bill's assurance, his plea really, that "Anybody who thinks we have done something wrong is wrong."

There is, needless to say, both truth and fiction in *Indians*, truth in its essence, fiction in its exaggeration and its eccentricity. The events Kopit recounts in flashback—the slaughter of the buffalo; the expedition of the Grand Duke Alexis; Cody's appearance on the stage; the success of his Wild West Show and Sitting Bull's appearance with it; Sitting Bull's assassination and the Wounded Knee massacre; the commission at Standing Rock—were all realities, not figments of the playwright's imagination. And they provide instances where all can be on the side of the angels. I suspect, however, that Kopit may have been in search of something more, of the hypocrisy he sees in the American life-style, of the displaced values he finds at its core. And they are far more difficult to present, occasionally do lead him to offer those good guys and bad guys and black-and-white interpretations, where the truth, the reality, is only mottled gray. We are left with a play that is right about its subject— about its Indians—but overstated and hazy in its extensions. It is too bad, because for America today it is those extensions that matter. We have long since failed the Indians, and it is something we can only indict, never in any way recall, despite our periodic outbreaks of good intentions.

Even when viewed exclusively as theatre, *Indians* should somehow have a greater cumulative effect, should move us more, if only because we are so very willing to be moved. For whatever reason—its diffuseness most of all—it remains a play more successful in some of its moments than it eventually is in its totality, with a structure and a development that are far too erratic to be fully satisfying. Fragmented and powerful, dazzling and annoying, it remains a work in the realm of the might-have-been, one whose realization on stage has yet to achieve the potential of its idea or the fulfillment of its aspiration. If that can be said of any drama that does not truly "work," it remains perhaps more true of *Indians* than of most.

PART TWO:
THE THEATRE
GOES TO WAR

God, unchanging, heart-sick-
en'd, shuddering,
Gathereth the darkness of the
night sky
To mask his paling counte-
nance from
The blood dance of His self-
slaying children.

The Silver Tassie

When Sean O'Casey's impassioned antiwar play *The Silver Tassie* was revived by Britain's Royal Shakespeare Company in 1969, one reviewer sensibly remarked of it, "Only O'Casey could have written [it] and probably only Yeats could have rejected it."* But reject it the sage of the Abbey Theatre did, provoking the first of many controversies—political, religious, theatrical—that were to surround the play for years to come.

It is, as Hugh Leonard has observed, a "bad, a terrible play. Perversely, but not incompatibly, it is also a masterpiece." More accurately, perhaps, it is a bad play during its first, third, and much of its fourth act, and a masterpiece in its second. That second redeems the play, not by lifting it beyond criticism, but by rendering the critic a pygmy flinging number-two pencils at a giant.

The Silver Tassie is an amalgam of styles and moods, ranging from realism and farce to allegory and symbolism. It moves

*Hugh Leonard, *Plays and Players*, November, 1969, pp. 20-23.

from a setting reminiscent of *Juno and the Paycock* and *The Plough and the Stars* to an expressionistically conceived battlefield in France, from comedy set-pieces to a tragically ironic plea against war and its senselessness. It is a play that very likely defies fully successful production and yet, in the moments when it works, makes one almost forgive it for all the rest.

Harry Heegan is about to go off to war—but not before he leads his Avondale Football Club to yet one more victory, the triumph that will permit them to retire the cup, the silver tassie. Two aging Dubliners, Harry's father, Sylvester, and his friend Simon Norton, are sitting by the fire waiting for his return. They talk and they argue; make life difficult for Sylvester's careworn wife, a woman older than he and already "stiffened with age and rheumatism"; taunt and are lectured by Susie Monican, a girl of twenty-two whose "tambourine theology" and "unflinching and uncompromising modesty" imprison her as much as they antagonize those who suffer them. Sylvester, however, has an explanation for Susie's religiosity. It is "adoration." It is, he tells Simon, adoration "accordin' to the flesh. . . . She fancied Harry and Harry fancied Jessie, so she hides her rage an' loss in the love of a scorchin' Gospel."

Meanwhile, they are getting a bit nervous about Harry's failure to return from the football match. It has been over for hours and Harry already has overstayed his leave. "If he misses now the tide that's waitin', he skulks behind desertion from the colours."

To what will be his sorrow, Harry is not about to miss the tide. He is twenty-three, tall, athletic, and given to the boisterous. To shouts of "Up Harry Heegan and the Avondales!" he comes striding in triumphantly, his arm around Jessie Taite, who carries the silver cup, "elevated as a priest would elevate a chalice." It is, Harry joyously proclaims, a "sign of youth, sign of strength, sign of victory!" And Harry has kicked the winning goal. Within a few hours of his triumph, in love, and glorying in his young manhood, Harry Heegan is off to war.

Almost from the first, there is a curious lack of dimension to the characters, a carelessness in construction that borders on indifference. It is almost as if O'Casey cared too much about some of it to care sufficiently about the rest. Yet, as J. C.

70

Trewin has written in an introduction, it is "a play in which O'Casey knew precisely what he wanted to do, and how to do it: to show the horror of war and its aftermath."

It is in the second act that he begins.

In the "jagged and lacerated ruin" of what was once a monastery in the war zone, Barney Bagnal, a buddy of Harry's who appears briefly in the first act, is tied in cruciform to a gun-wheel, being punished for a "regimental misdemeanor." Almost directly opposite is a shell-damaged, life-size crucifix, its Christus hanging forward with arms outstretched toward a stained-glass figure of the Virgin. Dominating all is a huge howitzer, its long barrel pointing front. Above and off to one side is The Croucher. His clothes are covered with mud and splashed with blood, and his face resembles a death's head. As the rain falls, he begins to intone:

> And the hand of the Lord was upon me, and carried me out in the spirit of the Lord, and set me down in the midst of a valley.

> And I looked and saw a great multitude that stood upon their feet, an exceeding great army.

> And he said unto me, Son of man, can this exceeding great army become a valley of dry bones?

And God asked him to prophesy, and he prophesied, "and the breath came out of them, and the sinews came away from them, and behold a shaking, and their bones fell asunder, bone from his bone, and they died, and the exceeding great army became a valley of dry bones."

A group of soldiers comes trooping in, wet and cold and weary. Why are they there, they wonder. There will, of course, be no answer and, as Barney sings "We're here because we're here," they begin to drift off to sleep.

But not for long. The corporal brings in a portly visitor, a civilian dressed in semimilitary garb, who is anxious to "penetrate a little deeper into danger." It may be foolish, but "it's an experience." A moment later a staff officer enters, prim and self-important, his uniform braid glittering, and issues a point-less order about a lecture on the "habits of those living between

71

Frigid Zone and Arctic Circle." He then departs as quickly as he came, followed shortly thereafter by the corporal with his V.I.P.

There is little that is really extraordinary in the language; what is remarkable is the conception that lifts it to memorable power. Stretcher-bearers come in carrying the wounded. They carry some of them toward the Red Cross station at the side, leave others on the ground outside. The wounded begin their ironically rendered plain song, a sort of mock-Gregorian chant:

> Carry on, carry on to the place of pain,
> Where the surgeon spreads his aid, aid, aid.
> And we show man's wonderful work, well done,
> To the image God hath made, made, made,
> And we show man's wonderful work, well done,
> To the image God hath made!

As they lie and loll about, battered, crippled, dying, their futures sacrificed to the god who goes by the name of War, they are wry and bitter. They are almost caricatures of Henry's men on the eve of Agincourt, reminders of the futility and of the "glory" that men once thought, and some perhaps still do think, is war. With its choral chanting, its repetition and dignity, its symbolism and its litany, there is a feeling almost of ritual— ritual in the face of a god whose existence in itself sometimes seems to challenge God.

The corporal returns and announces that the enemy is attacking. "Let us honour that in which we do put our trust." They group around the gun.

CORPORAL: Dreams in bronze and dreams in stone have gone
To make thee delicate and strong to kill.

SOLDIERS: We believe in God and we believe in thee. . . .

CORPORAL: Tear a gap through the soul of our mass'd enemies;
Grant them all the peace of death;

72

Blow them swiftly into Abram's bosom,
And mingle them with the joys of paradise!

SOLDIERS: For we believe in God and we believe in
thee.

The enemy has broken through. They swing the gun around and
shove a shell into the breech and begin to fire. Soon, there are
only the searchlights and the flashes of the gun against a darkening
sky.

Trewin has said of his first viewing of this second act that
"nothing had brought war more fiercely to the English stage
since the soldier Williams in *Henry V* had spoken by the camp-
fire in the daybreak of Agincourt: ' . . . When all those legs, and
arms, and heads, chopp'd off in the battle, shall join together at
the latter day. . . .' " And it is true.

It is sentimental, almost maudlin, in its way. But in its effect
it is extraordinary, evoking an image of the absurdity of war
that is far more powerful in its impact than countless more
recent antiwar plays and films, an image that in its very aban-
donment of realism, its heightening of the very "lie"* that is
the theatre, conveys its truth. As Robert Speaight, the actor-
writer who was one of the few Irish Catholics to defend the
play at the time of its Dublin premiere in 1935, wrote in the
Catholic Herald, O'Casey had "seen into the heart of the horror
of war and wrenched out its dreadful secret: that the co-heirs of
Christ destroy one another in the sight of the Son of Man."

What comes after is almost anticlimactic. Harry Heegan has
been returned home to a hospital, where a bit too coincidentally, Sylvester and Simon are patients and Susie Monican is
a nurse's aide. Susie has changed, if the two cronies have not.
Now her attractiveness is obvious—in her short and smartly cut
skirt, in her newfound sense of importance, in her manner.
Harry, too, has changed. He has lost the use of his legs and
propels himself about in his wheelchair. He is embittered, filled

*The word is Laurence Olivier's, at a press conference at Canada's Expo
'67. It could not be more accurate.

with self-pity and, says Sylvester—who could as easily be a casual acquaintance as his father, for all O'Casey makes of the relationship—he is "always thinking of Jessie."

Jessie, however, has abandoned him in favor of Barney Bagnal, who saved his life on the battlefield. Harry, who is to have an operation in the morning, has almost despaired. Angry, resentful, and tormented, he tells Susie:

> In a net I'll catch butterflies in bunches; twist and mangle them between my fingers and fix them wriggling on to mercy's banner. I'll make my chair a Juggernaut, and wheel it over the neck and spine of every daffodil that looks at me, and strew them dead to manifest the mercy of God and the justice of man!

But his rage and his self-pity do not matter. He is left to cry out: "God of miracles, give a poor devil a chance, give a poor devil a chance!"

But God does not and the doctors cannot give Harry a chance. The operation does not succeed and the last act finds him, still in his wheelchair, even more embittered, even more furious with fate and those around him, a guest at the football club dance. He follows Jessie and Barney about, angrily challenging a world that has left him with legs that "can neither walk, nor run, nor jump, nor feel the merry motion of a dance."

There is nothing of the stiff-upper-lip about Harry, and even his family and friends regret his presence at the dance. It is no good for him and it is a burden for them.

> SIMON: To carry life and colour to where there's nothing but the sick and helpless is right; but to carry the sick and helpless to where there's nothing but life and colour is wrong. . . .
>
> SYLVESTER: To bring a boy so helpless as him, whose memory of agility an' strength time hasn't flattened down, to a place wavin' with joy an' dancin', is simply, simply——
>
> SIMON: Devastating, I'd say.

For Harry, it is precisely that. Only Teddy, a neighbor blinded in the war, would not prefer to avoid him. To the others he is an embarrassment, a reminder of his past who can only be a shadow of it.

Harry is not one to suffer in silence. He tells them to get him the cup, that he will "mind it here" until they are ready to drink to the Avondales from it—as he and Jessie once drank. When he does prepare to drink from it, he says he will have red wine:

> red like the faint remembrance of the fires in France;
> red wine like the poppies that spill their petals on the
> breasts of the dead men. No, white wine, white like
> the stillness of the millions that have removed their
> clamours from the crowd of life. No, red wine; red
> like the blood that was shed for you and for many for
> the commission of sin!

A moment later, he wheels about in his chair to the beat of the music being played by the band. Then, alone with the sightless Teddy, laments: "I never felt the hand that made me helpless."

TEDDY: I never saw the hand that made me blind.

HARRY: Life came and took away the half of life.

TEDDY: Life took from me the half he left with you.

HARRY: The Lord hath given and the Lord hath taken away.

TEDDY: Blessed be the name of the Lord.

Harry is asked to sing a Negro spiritual for them, to play his ukulele as he once did. But they are unthinking, uncaring. They—his family included—dash out in mid-song to where the balloons are being released. Left alone, Harry again picks up the silver tassie and wheels himself out into the garden with it. When he returns, it is to rail against his fate:

> Dear God, this crippled form is still your child.
> Dear mother, this helpless thing is still your son.

Harry Heegan, me, who, on the football field,
could crash a twelve-stone flyer off his feet.
For this dear Club three times I won the Cup,
and grieve in reason I was just too weak this year to
play again. And now, before I go, I give you all the
Cup, the Silver Tassie, to have and to hold for ever,
evermore.

And he holds it out to them, "mangled and bruised as I am
bruised and mangled. Hammered free from all its comely
shape." He flings it, crushed and useless, to the floor. And then
he leaves, echoing Teddy's acknowledgment that their best is all
behind them, but, "What's in front we'll face like men!"

It is all, says Susie, part of the "misfortune of war," and it
will happen so long as wars are waged.

In creating a gallery of the cruel, the indifferent, and the
callous, a gallery of virtual caricatures, against which to play out
Harry's tragedy—the tragedy of war—O'Casey in the end goes
too far. The very exaggeration of their indifference in the face
of his anguish becomes a barrier. Harry's own cry of rage against
the futility and waste of war is eloquent and moving, but it is
that second act that remains, that almost defies and certainly
disarms, criticism. It is it that stands out among so much else
that is flawed, erratic, and almost carelessly thrown together as
an unforgettable image; it that almost enables *The Silver Tassie*
to say what perhaps cannot be said.

What is it? I want to know
what it is. The thing that
Sergeant saw to make him
know to shoot that kid and
old man. I want to have it,
know it, be it.

The Basic Training of Pavlo Hummel

A radio is softly playing American pop records and a young
American soldier in sunglasses and fatigues stands drinking a
beer in a Saigon whorehouse. Upstage, a Vietnamese girl is getting another bottle from a cooler. Another American sits with a
girl on his lap, and yet another with his head drooping. Off to
one side, observer rather than participant, in beribboned dress
uniform, is a young black soldier. Without warning, a hand
flashes briefly and there is the sound of a loud clump on the
floor. "Grenade!" shouts Pavlo Hummel, grabbing for it. But
before he can throw it away from them, there is an explosion.
In an instant, all but the black soldier, Ardell, lie dead or dying.

ARDELL: That the way it happen sometimes, Pavlo.
   Everybody hit, everybody hurtin', but the radio ain't
   been touched, the dog didn't feel a thing. . . . Get off
   it, Pavlo. Bounce on up here!

And Pavlo snaps to attention. A moment later, restored to
life for the flashback that is David Rabe's *The Basic Training of
Pavlo Hummel*, he is back at Fort Gordon, being harangued by

77

Sergeant Tower, a black drill sergeant. Pavlo Hummel, young, white, from 231 East 45th Street in Manhattan, has begun his basic training.

Pavlo is a confused and quirky kid, quixotic and eager to please, anxious to find his manhood. He moves through basic training, lying to his fellow trainees about his exploits as a car thief, anxiously preparing for the proficiency test that comes at the end of his eight weeks of training, gung-ho about being a soldier, yet anything but a brutal, hard-nosed killer.

First Sergeant Tower bullies, exhorts, and cajoles his rookies from a high platform, putting them through their drills, extolling the merits of duty-honor-country. And Pavlo, mixed-up, eager, oddball, eats it up. Returning to camp after a five-mile, double-time run, he begins to do push-ups. To the obvious annoyance of his platoon, especially of a recruit named Kress:

> Hummel, you're crazy. You really are.... I hate crazy people. I hate 'em. YOU ARE REALLY CRAZY, HUMMEL. STOP IT OR I'LL KILL YOU.

Pavlo has other problems as well. He has gone too far with the tales about his prowess as a car thief. When a billfold disappears, his fellow recruits accuse him of stealing it and of making off with a total of $312 of their money. Obviously, his moment of reckoning is coming. But before it arrives, he meets a corporal recently returned from Vietnam, who fires his eagerness for action. The corporal tells of how his squad leader got the better of the Vietcong one day when they encountered an old man and a little girl coming toward them:

> I'm next to the Sarge and he tells this ole boy to stop, but they keep comin' like they don't understand, smilin' and wavin', so the Sarge says for 'em to stop in Vietnamese and then I can see that the kid is cryin'.... And Tinden, right then, man he dropped to his knees and let go two bursts—first the old man, then the kid, cuttin' them both right across the face....

PAVLO: I don't know why he shot . . . them.

At this point in almost any other play about Vietnam there would have been a predictable outcome: the Vietnamese would have been searched and found innocent of harboring any concealed weapons, just two more victims of American malfeasance in Indochina. Rabe's view is more complex, less relentlessly polemical. He is concerned more with the *why* of how men act than with one-dimensional point-scoring. These Vietnamese *were* carrying TNT in satchel charges, enough of it "to blow up this whole damn state. . . . Been around; so he knew." Pavlo is awed. It leaves him convinced of one thing: "What is it? I want to know what it is. The thing that Sergeant saw to make him know to shoot that kid and old man. I want to have it, know it, be it."

It is, however, only an interlude. When he returns to the barracks, he is pounced upon, beaten, and kicked by Kress and the others, bent on revenge for his supposed thefts—and for his being Pavlo. Pavlo, his platoon leader tells him, is "sometimes . . . unbelievable." But Pavlo has his reasons, even his reasons for having legally changed his name:

> Someday, see, my father's gonna say to me, "Michael,
> I'm so sorry I ran out on you," and I'm gonna say,
> "I'm not Michael, asshole. I'm not Michael anymore."

Meanwhile, he has one concern: "They're gonna mess with me—make a clerk outa me or a medic or truck driver, a goddamn moron—or a medic—a nurse—a fuckin' WAC with no tits—or a clerk, some little goddamn twerp of a guy with glasses and no guts at all."

And, just like that, Pavlo decides to kill himself by sniffing airplane glue and swallowing a bottle of aspirin. But it doesn't work. He is revived and, basic training over, it is time to go home on a furlough. He and Ardell, the voice in his head, observer and adviser, conscience and goad, the man who has told him he's "black on the inside," decide to do it up right. Donning his dress uniform and shades, he takes on a new and cocky identity. "You so pretty, baby, you gonna make 'em cry," Ardell tells him. "You tell me you name, you pretty baby!" Pavlo snaps to attention: "PAVLO MOTHERHUMPIN' HUMMEL!" In gear, he is the figure of his fantasies: tough, sure of himself, the potent lover.

And so Pavlo Hummel goes home, to his hotshot brother, Mickey, his psychotic mother, and a girl he finds has married someone else. He insists to Mickey: "I'm different! I'm different than I was! . . . I'm not an asshole anymore!" Mickey thinks he is "a goddamn cartoon."

Cartoon or no, Pavlo goes to Vietnam and, just as he had feared, is made a medic. One of those he encounters is Brisbey, who has been in the army for seventeen years and has been hit by a land mine. Brisbey has "no legs no more, no balls, one arm," and Brisbey is bent on one thing: he wants someone to kill him. "Some guys, they get hit, they have a stump," he tells Pavlo. "I am a stump."

But Pavlo refuses to kill him or to help him to die, and eventually he is called to the captain's office.

> PAVLO: I want to feel, sir, that I'm with a unit Victor Charlie considers valuable enough to want to get it. And I hope I don't have to kill anyone; and I hope I don't get killed.

And so, Pavlo gets his transfer.

All the while, a black soldier lies downstage, crying out in agony as his life ebbs away from a wound in his stomach. He is finished off by two darting black-garbed VC, who remove his pistol belt, flack vest, and wallet, then dash off into the night, as silent as they came.

Pavlo soon warms to his task, gets himself a couple of VC, and gets himself wounded as he is trying to retrieve the dead soldier's body. Ardell tells him:

> The knowledge comin' baby. I'm talking about what your kidney know, not your fuckin' fool's head. I'm talkin' about your skin and what it sayin', thin as paper. We melt; we tear and rip apart. Membrane, baby. Cellophane. Ain't that some shit.

When he is hit again, Pavlo begins to realize that war isn't

80

what it was cracked up to be in all those B-movies. Although Ardell tells him the second wound leaves him a choice, he elects to remain in Vietnam. He wants, Ardell says to him, to get "one more slopehead, make him know the reason why." When he is wounded again, he *does* want out. But now it's too late; Pavlo Hummel is going to die.

His death, however, is not to be at the hands of the Vietcong or the North Vietnamese, but at those of a jealous sergeant he insults and angers in a whorehouse. Four days, thirty-eight minutes later, the education of Pavlo Hummel is at an end. He has been zipped into a blue rubber bag and is being shipped home, yet another pointless death in a long since pointless war. What, Ardell challenges, does Pavlo think of it, of the war and the people back home who say he is a victim and an animal and a fool? "It all shit!" That is what Pavlo Hummel thinks of it.

David Rabe spent eleven months in Vietnam, an experience reflected not only in *Pavlo Hummel*, with its pathetic young misfit who eventually comes to the point where he can "look at the human wreckage and not relate to it," but also in the less fully realized *Sticks and Bones*, with its blind veteran who returns home to his uncomprehending Middle American family. But, unlike most of those who have written antiwar plays, Rabe refuses to grind the axe, to present pure victims and pure monsters. Although the army helps Pavlo to become a killer, it does so with his own eager cooperation. It does not "dehumanize" him, to use that much overused and generally meaningless word; it gives him the occasion to cultivate his basic capacity for the inhumane. At the end, Pavlo has, perhaps, achieved a partial self-identity, but the what or the why of that identity is never really clear. It is as if Rabe himself had not quite decided. Or perhaps that is the point. Perhaps the Pavlo of Act 1 and the Pavlo of Act 2 are really very much the same, neither hero nor villain, neither bad nor good guy, but a lonely, confused, and infinitely fallible man.

If the ambiguity of Pavlo is at times disturbing, there is a reverse of the coin that gives the play much of its impact and dimension. Rabe does not make anything—apart from the hell and absurdity of war—*that* black and white. He avoids both easy sentimentality and facile point-scoring and—and this, too, is a

81

welcome relief—he realizes that horror and comedy, like tragedy and comedy, are seldom far apart. His Vietcong are no more heroic than his Americans (which by now seems almost refreshing). It is war itself that becomes the horror story, a tragicomic nightmare in which no one really can win, in which casual cruelty and indifference are as likely to be found in the black pajamas of the Vietcong as in GI battle dress. It is that and the refusal to be simplistic, together with Rabe's ability to create pungent, evocative, and believable dialogue and unstereotyped characters, that lifts *Pavlo Hummel* above such agit-prop exercises as *Viet Rock*, *Pinkville*, and the rest and makes it, diffused focus and all, one of the best, if not the best play to come out of America's Vietnam nightmare.

All the words, writing, march-
ing, fasting, demonstrating —
all the peaceable acts of the
defendants, over a period of
some years — had failed to
change a single American
decision in Vietnam.

The Trial of the Catonsville Nine

Although Daniel Berrigan insists in his introduction to the published version of *The Trial of the Catonsville Nine* that he has
"worked directly with the data of the trial record, somewhat in
the manner of the new 'factual theatre,'" his play differs not
only from most plays produced by that theatre of fact, but
from most other courtroom dramas. It is more document than
documentary, more personal testimony than play. It does not
argue with the audience; it makes no revelations; it partakes of
no "reconstructions" or dramatizations of the events that lead
the nine defendants to where they are, the Baltimore Federal
Court, October, 1968, Judge Roszel Thomsen presiding. It
offers no hypertensive confrontations between court and defendants or defendants and prosecution. Yet it is surprisingly,
even intensely, dramatic, more so than many more deliberately
theatrical works. "I was saving my soul," says one of the defendants. "It was a choice between saving my soul and losing
it."

If that sounds melodramatic, perhaps it's just as well. We live
in a peculiarly melodramatic time and the American theatre

only infrequently takes account of it. Father Berrigan's play does. It dramatizes the possibility of reclaiming what we have professed are our ideals. It reminds us we are individuals capable of response, not merely numbers in an Internal Revenue Service (or FBI) file. Although it is a mediocre "play" by traditional standards, it is provocative politics and exceptional theatre.

The facts of the charge and the trial are well known. On May 17, 1968, Daniel and Philip Berrigan and seven others took 378 records from the files of the Catonsville, Maryland, draft board, poured homemade napalm over them, and set them afire. Then they looked on, praying, television cameras recording, for fifteen minutes while they waited for the police to arrive. They were brought to trial on October 7, 1968, in Baltimore, pleaded innocent, and were convicted of destroying government property and interfering with the operations of the Selective Service System.

Father Philip Berrigan, a member of the Society of St. Joseph, an Order founded after the Civil War to work with blacks, and, insofar as is known, the first priest to be tried, convicted, and imprisoned for a political crime, tells of the events that preceded not only the civil disobedience at Catonsville, but of the pouring of blood over draft files in the Baltimore Customs House seven months earlier:

> The military were immune
> from any citizen influence
> They were a law unto themselves
> General Wheeler ignored our letters
> So we went to his home
> and demonstrated outside
> We were forced to leave
> We came back in a month's time
> and were forced out again
> The third time   we were forcibly ejected

"How much time is left this country?" he speculates.

In one way or another, that is the question that plagues each of the defendants, all of them Roman Catholic: David Darst, the young Christian Brother of whom Philip Berrigan admits in

84

his *Prison Journals*, "We had suspicions of him as a religious 'snoop,' whose superpatriotism might have led him to infiltrate us for some branch of federal or military intelligence," but who they came to think "is quite too good to be true"; Marjorie and Thomas Melville, a nun and a priest who met while working with the poor in Guatemala, were ejected from the country, and subsequently married; Mary Moylan, who served as a nurse with the Women's Volunteer Association in Africa; John Hogan, a former Maryknoll Brother, who was ordered out of Guatemala by his Order at the same time as the Melvilles; George Mische, who worked with various foreign-aid programs in Latin America; and Thomas Lewis, a painter and active member of the civil rights and antiwar movements, articulate, agonized, and impassioned.

The judge asks Lewis what would have happened if the men whose records they'd destroyed had not been sent. Would there not have been others?

> But why your honor
> Why this?
> Why does it have to be like this
> You are accepting the fact
> that if these men are not sent
> other men will be sent
> You are not even asking
> what can be done
> to stop this insane killing

Berrigan's play is tendentious and at times simplistic. Perhaps simplistic. As each of the nine recounts how he came to his moment of decision, to "those four or five minutes when our past went up in flames," and the judge periodically reminds them they are not trying the problem of race in America, or the CIA, the United Fruit Company, open occupancy, the history of the world in the twentieth century, the Roman Catholic bishops of the United States ("Unfortunately," says one), or the air war in Vietnam, Berrigan builds his case, his indictment of the system that led to and perpetuated the American involvement in Vietnam, "the land of burning children."

85

The deck, of course, is stacked, as at the moment it perhaps had to be. Whether one labeled Daniel Berrigan a "self-righteous fanatic" leading a collection of "protesting rabble," as another prominent American writer-priest did, or considered the war in Vietnam a "criminal assault on the people of Indochina," as Noam Chomsky contended in an answering essay, had become largely a question of rhetoric.

Daniel Berrigan is the last of the defendants to testify and, predictably, the poet-priest is the most eloquent. He tells of how his brother's earlier pouring of blood on draft files caused him to reflect that "from the beginning of our republic/ good men had said no/ acted outside the law/ when conditions so demanded," and that the actions of such men might in time be not only vindicated, but shown to be lawful, "a gift to society, a gift to history and to the community." The defense asks:

Was your action at Catonsville a way of carrying out your religious beliefs?

DANIEL BERRIGAN: Of course it was
May I say
if my religious belief is not accepted
as a substantial part of my action
then the action is eviscerated
of all meaning   and I should be
committed for insanity

Berrigan recounts how his views on the war took shape; how, together with Howard Zinn, he went to Hanoi early in 1968 to receive three captured American pilots the North Vietnamese had promised to release to "the American peace movement" and there underwent an American bombing attack:

So I went to Catonsville
and burned some papers   because
the burning of children
is inhuman and unbearable
I went to Catonsville
because I had gone to Hanoi

86

As the defense concludes its presentation, Berrigan is asked to read the meditation he had composed to accompany the statement issued by the nine defendants:

Our apologies   good friends
for the fracture of good order   the burning of paper
instead of children   the angering of the orderlies
in the front parlor of the charnel house
We could not   so help us God   do otherwise

The time is past, he says, "when good men may be silent."

It was, as Philip Berrigan acknowledged in his *Prison Journals*, a "complex though legally hopeless trial," in which the government set out to prove only what the defendants not only already admitted but celebrated. "This trial does not include the issue of the Vietnam conflict," the prosecution maintains in its summation. Rather, it insists, it is concerned only with the defendants' destruction of government property. On that basis only, the jury is enjoined to reach a verdict.

The defense counters with the assertion that it is not a question of "records which are independent of life," that their burning was "a symbolic act" intended to impede a system they held was "immoral, illegal, and is destroying innocent people around the world." It is, of course, a plea that the jury decide the case not on the basis of the "facts" presented by the government but on the basis of conscience.

JUDGE: This morning, I said to you that if you attempt
   to argue that the jury has the power to decide this
   case on the basis of conscience, the court will inter-
   rupt to tell the jury their duty. The jury may not
   decide this case on the basis of the conscience of the
   defendants. They are to decide this case only on the
   basis of the facts presented by both sides.

There is no echo to inquire what are facts and what is truth.

After the jury files out, the judge grants the request of the defendants to be heard by the court. "I do not want to cut them off from anything they may want to say."

As Daniel Berrigan presents him, Judge Roszel Thomsen seems an honest, a sympathetic, a compassionate man. He also seems a bemused one, his own best instincts under challenge, his faith in the law a bulwark but not in the end a defense. "As a man," he says, "I would be a very funny sort if I were not moved by your sincerity on the stand, and by your views. I agree with you completely, as a person." But, he continues,

> a variety of circumstances make it most difficult to have your point of view presented. It is very unfortunate, but the issue of the war cannot be presented as sharply as you would like. The basic principle of our law is that we do things in an orderly fashion. People cannot take the law into their own hands.

But, George Mische insists, "Change could come if one judge would rule on the war." The judge demurs, suggesting that he misunderstands "the organization of the United States," and that a single judge ruling on it would not end the war. "Each judge must do his best with what comes before him."

They ask the judge if they may conclude with a prayer, the Our Father, in which members of the court join, after which the jury—a jury that had been told, apparently to its satisfaction, perhaps to its relief, that "the law does not recognize political, religious, moral convictions, or some higher law, as justification for the commission of a crime, no matter how good the motive may be"—returns with its verdict. Each of the nine is found guilty on three counts: destruction of government property, destruction of Selective Service records, and interference with the Selective Service Act of 1967.

Speaking for the defendants, Daniel Berrigan utters the play's concluding lines:

> We would simply like to thank the Court and the prosecution. We agree that this is the greatest day of our lives.

After which, in production, a film of the actual napalming of the files was shown—a film with, Philip Berrigan notes in his account of the trial, "an interesting history," since prior to the trial it had been kept off the air by government threats to prosecute the station for conspiracy. "We did this to make it more difficult for people to kill one another," one of the nine asserts.

Daniel Berrigan has one great advantage over most other writers of political drama: he is a poet. Even in its New York version, somewhat revised by Saul Levitt, it was the poet's eye, the poet's ability to select, to convey an image, that prevailed. His lines have a resonance where others' frequently are earthbound; he can evoke, where they usually can only expound. It was, Berrigan says in describing his hope in culling and condensing the twelve hundred pages of the trial record, "to induce out of the density of matter an art form worthy of the passionate acts and words of the Nine."

That is not to say he can, or could convince or that the play could change minds any more than the Catonsville Nine could move mountains. In saying there are higher laws than the laws of the land, a law "taking precedent over human law," and that it is to this that man owes his ultimate loyalty, the play, like the defendants, adheres to one American tradition and violates another. It is a statement, not an argument, and it does not suggest that the audience take a stand but, rather, that it is, or should be, impossible *not* to. When the judge muses, "This is the first case in which the issue of conscience has been brought up in my courtroom," it is not merely an indictment of a system but of a people who take that system for granted.

One may believe in what the antiwar Protestant theologian Robert McAfee Brown calls "the allegiance one is called upon to give to a structured fabric in our society" and be convinced that the Catonsville Nine were engaged in an effort to rend that fabric. One also might consider it an effort to mend it. Whichever the case, it seems impossible to deny that, at Catonsville, nine men and women acted in terms of their consciences—those consciences ruled irrelevant in an American court of law—and that *The Trial of the Catonsville Nine* challenges each member of the audience to examine his own. It would be difficult indeed to find a more significant role for the theatre to perform. As Daniel Berrigan said in a letter to the SDS Weathermen,

"The times demand not that we narrow our method of communication but that we actually enlarge it if anything new or anything better is going to emerge."

This mighty enemy
follows in the footsteps
of all our previous
oppressors. . . .
We will outlive
him *too*
Time is on our side

Vietnam Discourse

Although several years have passed since he made the observation, there is no reason to think Peter Weiss has abandoned his conviction that "art should be so strong that it changes life," that "otherwise it is a failure." Weiss has sought to achieve such an art in play after play, but never elsewhere with the ambitiousness of *Vietnam Discourse.** In it he has attempted something truly extraordinary—the encompassing of 2,500 years of a country's history in a cohesive revolutionary statement. But the genius that would require is nowhere in evidence. What is is a playwright committed to the theatre as an organ for political and social change. Regrettably, the two are a world apart.

Technically and stylistically, *Vietnam Discourse* is Weiss's most complex play thus far. It is also his most poetic, an at times curious blend of highly stylized writing and agit-prop

---

* *Discourse on the Progress of the Prolonged War of Liberation in Vietnam and the Events Leading Up to It as Illustration of the Necessity for Armed Resistance Against Oppression and on the Attempts of the United States of America to Destroy the Foundations of Revolution.*

91

rhetoric which employs chorus and choreography, an elaborate structure with characters who are at one moment anonymous representatives of their epoch, at another specific figures in history. "The aim is to present figures bound up in historical processes, even when it is a matter of historical developments of which the participants were themselves not aware," Weiss says in the introduction. "An attempt is made to present a succession of social stages, with all their essential features and discrepancies, in such a way that they throw light on the conflict existing today."

In making the transition from one role to another, from era to era, the fifteen actors dispense with costume changes in favor of simple black or white uniform-style attire. They effect their change in identity by means of such attributes as weapons, helmets, shields, shawls, shoulder straps, military caps and decorations, and flags. Beyond this, the changes in role are indicated by changes in position, groupings, or manners of speech. The Vietnamese and representatives of feudal China wear black, the colonial powers and their vassals white.

In Part I, Weiss portrays in eleven "phases" the evolution of Vietnam from approximately 500 B.C. to 1953, a period that began with the appearance of Chinese mariners in the south of what is today Vietnam and ended with the first air landing of French troops at Dien Bien Phu. It was marked by regular invasions, usurpations, domination, and exploitation—by the Chinese, the French, the British, the Japanese. All that changed was the name or the nationality of the exploiter and the words of the chorus in phase 1 could stand as a description of it almost until the end:

> The land of our fathers
> was invaded by strangers
> Our fathers sought a new land
> We live in the land that our fathers found
> The land of our fathers is invaded by strangers
> Our fathers see the junks of the strangers
> sail out fully laden
> The sacrificial dishes on the graves of our fathers
> stand empty

92

Our fathers summon us
to free our land from the strangers

With the end of World War I, revolutionary fervor has begun to stir. It is given impetus by accounts of the Russian Revolution, brought to Vietnam by sailors, reports of "a country where the workers have seized power," a country that was backward and whose peasants were enslaved, a country where the workers were inexperienced and uneducated, but where "their passion and their courage were great." A country at least in some ways not unlike their own. What, the peasants wonder, would happen if *they* rose up, if they went to the house of the factory owner, to the plantation office, to the governor's residence, taking their hungry children with them, to make their own demands? The chorus has the answer:

For thousands of years they bore the oppression
seeking their liberty in rebellion
And liberty meant for them
freedom from debt and more land to plough
And this each new leader promised them

Each new leader promised, and each new leader reneged.

By now, some—among them Nguyen Ai Quoc (Ho Chi Minh)—have grown tired of listening to those promises. In 1941 they found the Viet Minh and, in 1944, the Vietnamese Liberation Army. By 1954, despite American aid to the French, Dien Bien Phu has fallen and the Geneva agreement already is being violated.

In Part II, poetry gives way almost entirely to polemic and the play becomes more obviously Brechtian, with a slide projector to show the various historical personages Weiss purports to portray and a loudspeaker to announce their names. From the moment it begins, it is clear there is to be no attempt at acknowledging any areas of gray in the behavior of the Americans: they are motivated solely by a cynical desire for self-aggrandizement and a blind anti-Communism, are but another—and perhaps the worst—in the long line of warlords and colonial powers with whom the Vietnamese people have had to contend.

93

Phase 1 depicts a "secret conference" in the Department of State, on April 3, 1954. John Foster Dulles is there to report on President Eisenhower's desire to sanction the relief of the French troops at Dien Bien Phu by American naval and air forces. Other political and military leaders speak out not merely in support of aiding the French but of other, perhaps more compelling reasons for intervention:

> The spread of Communism
> to the countries of Indochina
> would be a serious threat
> to the free world
> . . . .
>
> Our strategic aim
> is to build a chain of bases
> around the Russia-China bloc
> . . . .
>
> We've been thinking
> of dropping a few small atom bombs
> which would work out cheaper
> than ground forces

Lyndon Johnson, then Senate minority leader, protests that no operations in Indochina should be undertaken without consultation with other nations and questions why the matter has not been put before the United Nations. He is told there is no time and that things already are in motion. There is a touch of irony to his insistence that there is no state of emergency that "would justify the President involving the country in warlike actions without the approval of Congress." The chorus observes:

> But inevitably the day will come
> when Congress will grant the President
> absolute authority
> to take all steps
> which he considers vital
> for the defense of freedom

94

That president will, of course, be Lyndon Johnson, the very man who voiced the protest.

Weiss shows Eisenhower addressing the nation on television, the Senate debating, the National Security Council in secret session. It is with the NSC meeting that trouble really sets in. Initially, there is the manner in which the participants are introduced over the loudspeaker. The secretary of the treasury is not a former industrialist but *the* chairman of the board of a coal and steel company. He immediately begins to discourse on what we import from Indochina and the desirability of controlling production there. When the secretary of defense speaks, it is as *the*, not the former, president of General Motors. Nelson Rockefeller, then coordinator of Inter-American Affairs, is described as co-owner of Standard Oil and "owner of the Chase Manhattan Bank." And so on down the line, as one industrialist and financier after another reveals the corruption and venality of his motives and proclaims the need to protect private investments, control the price of raw materials, ensure customary profit margins, and increase American defense expenditures. On occasion, Weiss, perhaps having failed to do his homework, supplies his speakers with a political rhetoric and frame of reference that are clearly alien to the American politician, who, if nothing else, is a master of the art of obfuscation, experienced in the techniques of convincing not only others, but himself of the rightness of his cause. It is the sort of dialog that at times would seem more at home in a satire than in a straight drama.

Business and industry have a pervasive role in American society and Weiss is entitled to his anticapitalist brief. Whether he is equally entitled to his misrepresentations and misstatements of fact is more problematical. For example, detailing Ngo Dinh Diem's early grooming by the Americans, a speaker refers to the future prime minister as living for "his first two years in the States . . . as a guest with Cardinal Spellman," when in fact he resided at the seminaries of the Maryknoll Order in Ossining, New York, and Lakewood, New Jersey, spoke throughout the country and, under Spellman's wing, pleaded his case in Washington. A bit later, someone asserts: "It is now July nineteen fifty-four/ the date laid down in Geneva/ for the holding of elections/ in both parts of Vietnam." The Geneva cease-fire

95

accord itself was signed on July 21, 1954; the elections were to be held two years later, in July, 1956. Such misrepresentations or misstatements are not only unfortunate, but unnecessary: the realities are damning enough.

Obviously, no playwright should be the prisoner of history. It would make the theatre a poorer place indeed. The theatre of *fact*, however, does not offer quite the same freedom. *Richard III* was not defended as historically accurate, nor did Schiller claim that Mary Stuart and Elizabeth I actually had the meeting that is the high point of *Mary Stuart*. The theatre of fact makes different and sterner demands.

Dramatically, there is something to be said for making America's Vietnamese misadventure seem a well thought-out play which progressed through a predetermined series of steps, all inspired by a desire to achieve ill-gotten political and economic gains. At least it lends the foreign policy of the time a consistency its clearly evident and extensively documented hit-or-miss improvisation did not possess. It gives Part II a narrative focus the facts of history themselves deny.

As the various meetings proceed in Washington, London, Geneva, and Paris, events in Saigon and throughout Vietnam are taking their inexorable course. The refugees flow toward Saigon, Diem's regime becomes ever more repressive, the North progresses despite "thousands of villages laid waste." The pervasive hypocrisy and cynicism of the American policy-makers continues, with only occasional hints of discomfort over the corruption of the figures that policy itself supports: "It's all vanished into the pockets/ of government officials/ black marketeers and speculators."

At home in America, the chorus asserts:

> One man in three is poor
> under your system
> They live herded together
> in crumbling houses
> . Ignorance
> holds them down
> Anger is rising
> in the big cities

Your slum dwellers
march in thousands
through the streets
demanding the rights
which the men in power
refuse them

As a Marxist, Weiss takes a determinedly anticapitalist line.
He idealizes the peasant and the worker and abhors the representatives of a system he believes keeps them in a state of
subservience in order to fill the coffers of the rich, the proper-
tied, and the otherwise indifferent. But he fatally weakens both
his play and his polemic by a complete rejection of the fact that
history is as often the product of accidents and miscalculations
as of black-and-white contending forces. To shape a play around
the idea that it is exclusively the latter is to deny reality, to
pursue propaganda to a point where it belongs at a rally not in a
theatre.

Asked several years ago whether he thought the theatre
should be a "political forum," Weiss answered in the affirma-
tive, asserting that it should work "almost in the way that agit-
prop did, playing with non-professional actors, performing in
factories, on the street, in schools." That this is not the way
Weiss writes is beside the point. Even so, the statement suggests
two of the main reasons for *Vietnam Discourse*'s failure. The
first is the conflict between form and content, one appropriate
to the theatre, the other to the street or meeting hall. The
second is the difficulty involved in "changing life," which Weiss
insists should be the goal of art, when the audience is not first
allowed the initiative and the facts to make up, and perhaps to
change, its own mind. Denying that, a play can only become the
prisoner of its own polemic.

If everything goes well, there shouldn't be a single thing in Constantinople left alive. This is a mission we can be very proud of.

We Bombed in New Haven

Not so long ago, one of my acquaintances in the Broadway theatre cynically referred to a drama of a few seasons earlier as "the intellectual play to see that season." The play in question will go unmentioned if only because it constituted a sad reflection on the season. The opening of *We Bombed in New Haven*, a serio-comic play about war and the men who fight it, probably filled the same role for at least the first few months of the 1968-69 season. And that, equally, may have said something about it. What it said was hardly encouraging.

We Bombed in New Haven, originally presented by the Yale Repertory Company in December, 1967, was one of several attempts on the part of the Yale School of Drama and its Dean, Robert Brustein, to wed politics and the theatre. More importantly, it was the first play by Joseph Heller, author of the often dazzling *Catch-22*. Although considerably abetted—at least in theory—by the presence in the cast of Jason Robards, Jr., and Diana Sands, a Broadway production would have been highly problematical were it not for the great success of Heller's novel. As it turned out, the stars were at least part of the play's New York undoing.

Joseph Heller flew sixty missions as a Twelfth Air Force

99

combat bombardier during World War II. That experience provided the background for *Catch-22* and for its Captain Yossarian. ("He had decided to live forever or die in the attempt, and his only mission each time he went up was to come down alive.") It also provided the basis for the far more conventional *We Bombed in New Haven*. Heller himself has called the play a "sequel"; the Yale publicity people termed it a "surreal comedy of war." It wound up being a little of both and not enough of either. Reviewing the excellent Yale production, *Life* theatre editor Tom Prideaux described it as "potentially . . . the best war play of our own particular day." And that, regrettably, must be a commentary on something other than Mr. Heller's play—at least it was at the time. Far better plays have succeeded it, notably David Rabe's *The Basic Training of Pavlo Hummel.*

We Bombed in New Haven is set in "the theatre, city, and country in which the play is presented"; its time is "always the present, the exact day and hour at which the play is being performed." Within the first few minutes it is obvious that we are going to play Pirandello again. The stage is set to resemble an Air Force briefing room. The curtain rises on actors dressed in flight suits, toting props, and moving parts of the set. Supposedly taken by surprise, the airmen playing actors playing airmen are momentarily flustered at the premature rise of the curtain. They react in confusion and embarrassment at being caught setting the scene. Unfortunately, this sort of thing has been done a few times too often—and better. An attention-getting device the first time or two around, it is now more likely to prompt a "let's-get-on-with-it" response.

When the actors playing airmen playing actors playing airmen (or words to that effect) do get on with it, we find that they are about to be sent out on a new bombing mission. Starkey, a captain happy in his job (he can stay at the base), asks, "Well, Major? Where are they going today?"

MAJOR: Constantinople.

STARKEY: There is no Constantinople. It's Istanbul now.

MAJOR: I know that.

STARKEY: Then why are we going there? . . .

MAJOR (tapping his manuscript): Because it says so.

STARKEY: Is it dangerous?

MAJOR: Not for those who survive. For those who don't—well, I'd call that dangerous.

STARKEY: Will anybody be killed there?

(The Major nods.)

> And we just go on working. If somebody's going to die today, why must it be over something that doesn't even exist, like Constantinople? Why don't we at least call it *Istanbul?* At least that's a name worth dying for.

Since all this occurs within roughly the first five minutes, it seems reasonable to assume it is merely the prelude to a far fuller exploration of the play's antiwar theme, that Heller will offer some new insights or, if not that, at least bring to his play some of the originality he displayed in *Catch-22.* Maybe there will be another Yossarian. After all, one seemingly could draw something of enormous theatrical effectiveness—indeed, something of enormous importance—from the novel's "Men went mad and were rewarded with medals."

Five airmen—a cocky young sergeant, a slightly older corporal, a career private nearing sixty, another corporal, and an attentive private—are gathered before the two officers. With them are five others, billed as "Idiots," who are virtually silent throughout the play. As the fiction of actors playing airmen slowly begins to turn into a new reality, the actors begin to show their apprehension, to question the course of the script:

SINCLAIR: What are *you* scared about? I'm the one that has to be killed.

JOE: I'm a little scared also. I'm starting to get a little scared of all of them.

HENDERSON: I'm not.

BAILEY: Aren't you worried at all?

101

HENDERSON: Nah, not me. And should I tell you why? ... Because I'm not really a soldier, that's why.... I'm an *actor* ... playing the part of a soldier.... It's just a little game we're having here now. It's only a play, a show, a little entertainment, so let's not get carried away too far and forget who we *really* are.... This soldier I'm pretending to be never even lived, so how could I get killed?

Henderson will shortly change his tune. But, for the moment, the audience has been given its mild dose of Brechtian alienation. To confirm it, Henderson absentmindedly shakes a piece of the "wall." Eventually, the planes are ready to take off for Constantinople. It is, the major assures them, "a good mission.... If everything goes well, there shouldn't be a single thing in Constantinople left alive. This is a mission we can be very proud of." There is a good deal of this more or less gallows humor in *We Bombed in New Haven*, some of it very funny, almost funny enough to cloak the fact that there's not much else.

When they return from the bombing mission, Henderson reports the "death" of Sinclair, but hastens to remind Ruth, the Red Cross worker who is the play's lone female, that it's only a play. Ruth moves forward to address the audience: "Another young boy killed in a war. And all of you just sat there. It happened right now. Didn't you care? Doesn't it mean anything to you?"

We have arrived at the play's all too obvious message: the callousness of modern man to death in wars he now is able to view in twenty-one-inch living color, martini at his elbow, indifference in his heart. Whether the play succeeds is, therefore, contingent upon Heller's ability to move the audience to an acceptance of this. An intellectual if not an emotional acceptance, though ideally both. It is not an easy task and, oddly, it may be rendered all the more difficult by the fact that it so obviously is the truth.

Heller introduces two additional Pirandello-type characters: the sportsmen, a hunter and a golfer. They are the play's backers and they want to have a role in the play—to play the game of war, in other words. They take close-order drill with shotgun and golf club. The major tells them that the next to die will be Henderson, on the "mission to Minnesota." Henderson, in the meantime, has been unable to find the actor who had been playing Sinclair. He hears a bugle playings taps.

HENDERSON: About Sinclair.

STARKEY: There *was* no Sinclair. He never lived. He didn't die.

HENDERSON: Then who did we just bury?

STARKEY: Sinclair. But he wasn't real. It didn't happen.

HENDERSON: Why did we bury him?

STARKEY: Because he was killed.

HENDERSON: Where is the boy who was playing the soldier who was killed by accident just now—

STARKEY: Not by accident. There are no accidents.

HENDERSON: By accident. He was killed in my plane when one of his own bombs exploded, wasn't he? That's an accident. He used to be an actor about my own age. He was here a little while ago. He isn't here now.

STARKEY: He isn't supposed to be here. We don't need him any more. That's why we killed him.

After a bit more of this, Act 1 closes with a bizarre scene in which a basketball is thrown about from one actor to another, then replaced by a second basketball. Starkey next produces a football, then building blocks, rattles, plastic harmonicas, and pacifiers. Henderson reminds him, "We're not kids" and is told that in that case Starkey has just the game for them. He produces a toy time bomb. They play with it for a while, then the captain presents them with a second one; this one is real and it explodes in the wings. At the curtain, Starkey is taunting the audience with a third one—perhaps a toy, perhaps real.

Had Heller been able to build from this macabre scene, which

103

apart from the rather juvenile quality of the toying with the audience, is an effective one, *We Bombed in New Haven* might be quite a play. Instead, in Act 2 it erodes into an overwritten and overwrought example of message drama. The dead Sinclair is replaced by the very young brother of another of the airmen. ("They said that the younger they took me into the service, the better it would be for me. They said it would disrupt my life less if I got killed sooner.") The older airmen tell the boy about their experiences: the girls, the travel, the cities they have bombed—New Haven, Philadelphia, Boston, Amsterdam, Stockholm, Denver, and next, Minnesota.

STARKEY: You've got to go out now and destroy Minnesota before it's too late.

HENDERSON: Too late for what?

STARKEY: Well . . . too late to destroy it, I guess.

MAJOR: I want to blow Minnesota off the map before someone else does.

Henderson has read the script and knows he is to die on the next mission. He refuses to go and hides out with Ruth. When the two sportsmen, now graduated to MPs, come to get him, he is promised protection by Starkey. But Starkey fails him. Ordered back into uniform, Henderson tries to escape, only to be shot by the hunter. Starkey congratulates the actor—Henderson—on the way he played his big death scene, but there is no response. The fiction has become the reality; the game of war a game in which people get killed.

Heller might have been better off had he stopped there. Instead, he appends a weak and maudlin scene in which Starkey, who must find a replacement for the dead Henderson, someone else to die over Minnesota, is presented with his own son. Each time he rejects him and asks for another recruit the same nineteen-year-old son returns. There is a great deal of talk about why Starkey—who "had nineteen years to save me from this"—didn't do something earlier; but obviously it is all futile.

STARKEY: Major! They've got three hundred names on that list.

MAJOR: They all belong to him.

Starkey's son is sent to bomb Minnesota and the audience is reminded, "None of this, of course, is really happening. . . . Do you think that I would actually let my son go off to a war and be killed . . . and just stand here talking to you and do nothing?" Well, hardly, audience, not any more than you've done it to each succeeding generation.

There are just enough good things in *We Bombed in New Haven* to cause one to speculate on what might have been. Just enough powerful moments to induce consideration of how much better it would have been without the overkill, the banality and sentimentality, the often simplistic approach to a far from simple problem. Heller has said, "I don't like the theatre. I think it's a very limited medium. I hardly ever go. Even the few times you see something good it's never really *that* good. Drama critics are too generous. They over-praise things." Some of which is true, some of which is not (and some of which Heller later was to reconsider). At its best, theatre can have an immediacy and an impact unobtainable by other mediums. *We Bombed in New Haven* fell considerably short of it. At most, it served as a reminder of how little serious theatre there is. Joseph Heller is serious; it is too bad he is not, at least thus far, a better playwright. Or, perhaps, it is merely too bad that he did not recognize one of the most basic of all playwriting tenets: a play at the mercy of its thesis is a play almost automatically in trouble. Even when drama critics are, as they were in this case, "too generous."

I believe, Admiral, that you
cannot delegate responsibility.
I believe both of us know that.

Pueblo

More than most plays in the theatre of fact, Stanley R. Greenberg's *Pueblo* sticks *to* the facts, not embroidering, not creating
fictional side or principal characters, not attempting "reconstructions" of events that may or may not have occurred but
would serve to advance the playwright's point of view. Drawing
almost entirely upon material from the public domain—
newspaper accounts, television interviews, verbatim reports of
the congressional and naval hearings—it is far more "honest,"
far more straightforward than, say, *The Deputy*, *Inquest*, or
Soldiers; far less given over to propounding a thesis. It has all
the ingredients of superior drama: pursuit and capture on the
high seas; the conflict between two views of duty; the question
of responsibility; the demands of patriotism versus those of
survival; and a central figure who, if his thinking is in many
ways clichéd and lacking in imagination, nonetheless ultimately
proves atypical in the ranks of the military. Yet, in the end, it
does not quite achieve the impact it should have; it does not
quite ask the questions. The reasons for this go a long way
toward pointing up some of the major problems confronting
both the documentary drama and the theatre of controversy.

As the play opens, Commander Lloyd Mark Bucher is alone
on stage. He wears his dress blues, his campaign ribbons, his
submariner's insignia. On catwalks above him, various admirals

and generals move into place: members of the military court of inquiry that will judge him, omniscient gods in a situation that does not admit of omniscience. Flashbulbs explode into light and Bucher begins to answer the unheard questions of "a phantom press conference," to tell of his past: his boyhood at Father Flanagan's Boys Town, where he went in the summer of 1941; his football scholarship to the University of Nebraska; his marriage to a girl he met on a blind date at a homecoming game.

From the catwalk above him, the presiding officer, a beribboned admiral, intones the preliminaries of the court of inquiry, which will "investigate the circumstances relating to the seizure of the USS Pueblo, AGER 2, by North Korean navy vessels which occurred in Sea of Japan on January 23, 1968," and the subsequent detention of the ship, its officers, and crew. The court, he asserts, is authorized "to submit its findings of fact, opinion and recommendations to the convening authority and is instructed to recommend administrative or disciplinary action as appropriate."

Gradually, Greenberg begins to alternate between the two hearings and a dramatization of the actual events surrounding the Pueblo's capture. The chairman of the subcommittee of the House Armed Services Committee sets forth its intention to:

> ascertain the national security implications implicit in the loss of the USS Pueblo, the requirement for corrective action both administrative and legislative, and the requirement for possible changes in the Code of Conduct for military personnel captured by the enemy. We are deeply concerned with the chain of command and control. We are after facts.

As in Bucher's own account, *Bucher: My Story*, much is made of the age and condition of the ship, its inadequate navigational system, armaments, and destruct system for its secret electronic equipment and codes. Bucher apparently made generally disregarded requests for repairs or replacements of all of these. His apprehensions are, however, counterweighted by his pride in achieving his first command. "She was," he says, a small ship, "but only someone who has been given command

108

can understand the intense pride that an individual has in, in that ship." Even so, the Pueblo's mission of "naval surveillance and intelligence collection in support of high priority national intelligence objectives" would seem to have called for more than the bureaucratic indifference he generally met. Nor is it easy to understand why Bucher was never informed of the potential dangers he might face—that the North Koreans were at the time threatening retaliation for the encroachment on their territorial waters by American vessels—and why the mission was instead labeled "minimal risk." A congressman asks Admiral Thomas H. Moorer, Chief of Naval Operations, who it was who made the decision that it was safe to place the Pueblo off the shores of North Korea at a time when anyone who read the newspapers was aware of the constant threats and attacks from the North on the South.

MOORER: The procedure for establishing a mission of this kind is quite lengthy in the sense that it goes up the chain of command through the Pacific Fleet Commander, through the Commander in Chief, Pacific, and through the Joint Chiefs of Staff and to the Secretary of Defense.

CONGRESSMAN: I understand the chain of command, Admiral, but if you know would you state who it was?

MOORER: Well, I think, sir, that the final decision— First, let me say that this ship was operating on the high seas. That . . .

CONGRESSMAN: Did you make the decision on the Pueblo? . . .

MOORER: No, Congressman, I did not.

CONGRESSMAN: Do you know who did? . . .

MOORER: What I am trying to make clear is, Mr. Congressman, that no one single individual made the decision. The ship was under the unified commander, and under the fleet commander in chief, and under the operational commander for operational purposes. It was approved here in Washington.

109

CONGRESSMAN: Who approved it here in Washington?

MOORER: It was approved by the Joint Chiefs of Staff and in addition referred to the Secretary of Defense.

CONGRESSMAN: So the decision was at least approved by the Secretary of Defense at that time, is that correct?

MOORER: By his office, yes, sir. Whether he directly participated I have no way of knowing.

CONGRESSMAN: I believe, Admiral, that you cannot delegate responsibility. I believe both of us know that.

And that is the real question, at least one of the real questions, of the play: the government's responsibility for the mission—a responsibility obfuscated by the military bureaucracy—Bucher's responsibility toward his mission and his men; and the country's subsequent responsibility when they were first threatened, then captured.

As the reconstruction of the events of January 23, 1968, proceeds, Bucher becomes increasingly concerned with two things: the destruction of classified materials and the fate of his men. Still, he for a time remains convinced they will not actually be attacked; he has not even considered what he would do in such an eventuality. "The Navy rated our mission as minimal risk," he tells the presiding officer.

After the North Korean subchaser's signal, "Heave to or I will fire," is ignored, the firing on the Pueblo begins. Bucher and others are wounded and eventually the ship is taken prisoner.

MOORER: Congressman, this was a United States Navy ship operating on the high seas manned by U.S. sailors. No American ship has been seized on the high seas for one hundred and fifty years.

But the Pueblo was, with seemingly no effort on the part of the American naval or air forces to relieve or rescue her. There were, however, orders issued, General McKee insists; it was simply that time and darkness intervened.

CONGRESSMAN: Suppose in your judgment, and this is hindsight, your planes had been on the alert and reached the Pueblo in time to strike on her behalf. Do you think you could have changed the results of this tragic accident?

GENERAL McKEE: This is pure speculation, sir. I think one of three things would have happened: We would have changed it; I would have gotten my aircraft shot down; or we would have started another war.

In any case, no aid was forthcoming despite repeated pleas, and at 1:50 P.M. the Pueblo surrendered. Much of its classified material had not yet been destroyed.

The chairman of the congressional subcommittee asks whether the navy has a precedent on whether the ship or the crew should be saved. He is told by Admiral Johnson that "the Navy wants to save both."

CONGRESSMAN: That is motherhood and apple pie. But the question is, wasn't Commander Bucher obeying his orders if, in his judgment, he could only save his crew by *not* firing his guns?

JOHNSON: That, sir, would be the decision of the Captain, of the man in command on the spot. It was his responsibility.

With the capture of the Pueblo, the ball was back in the other court. It carried with it elements of the same question that confronted Bucher before his surrender. It soon becomes clear, at least as Greenberg presents it, that all the "on call" forces supposedly available to assist the ship were unavailable at the time they were needed, that we "had a contingency plan to use forces which did not exist!" Strictly speaking, this is not true; the forces did exist. It was other factors—time, implications, options—that resulted in their not being used.

Unable or unwilling, *at the time*, to come to the Pueblo's aid, the government was, in effect, confronted with the same question as Bucher: Which served the greater good, the saving of men or the sanctity of the mission? Was the credibility of the country—what remained of it—more important than the lives of the crew? Were the contingencies such that a rescue attempt might have escalated the situation into full-scale, perhaps nuclear, war? Out of his paternalism toward his men, Bucher decided one way. Out of the real or imagined requirements of national security, the government apparently decided the other.

When he is warned by the court counsel that he is now "suspect of a violation of the Uniform Code of Military Justice" because of his failure to resist and his subsequent confession, Bucher responds:

> I think there are inconsistencies in the Code of Conduct which was written for men at war, ground soldiers, under entirely different circumstances. I will say that the Navy left us there, left us at sea and left us in captivity, for nearly a year. I will say that we did as well as anyone under the circumstances, and better than most.

Bucher begins to tell of—and the play to dramatize—how he and his men were kicked and beaten and interrogated by the North Koreans, led by an officer nicknamed Super C. He relates how they were accused of being war criminals, spies for the CIA, and threatened with death if they did not confess. One of his officers observes, "I never thought the United States would let this happen to us:" That, perhaps, is the unanswered question.

Bucher is told that if he does not sign the confession his men will be shot one by one in his presence.

SUPER C: We will begin with the youngest first.

BUCHER: I was not prepared to see my crew shot. I was convinced they were animals. I was convinced they would do it. I knew they would kill my people so I told them . . . I'll sign . . . I'll sign . . . for the love of God I'll sign the God damn confession.

"After I confessed, I tried to drown myself in a bucket of

112

water in my room," he tells them. "I couldn't do it." During their subsequent months of imprisonment, he continues, he "determined that our resistance would be designed to fool and mock the Koreans in our phony confessions and letters and photographs home."

Their resistance took entirely passive forms—an officer urinating on a potted plant in order to kill it, nuances in their letters back home, recording their confessions in voices other than their own. Seemingly, there were no attempts at escape, no concentrated efforts at rebellion. Was it simply a matter of preserving their lives? Did some of the eighty-two members of the crew—the majority of whom had not known the nature of their mission—experience some sense of guilt over it? We will perhaps never know.

Pueblo, relying entirely upon existing documentation, refusing to hypothesize, does not explore the question. It is .one of its weaknesses, perhaps one of the limitations of documentary drama overall, that to have done so would have been a violation of its own ground rules. It points toward what is probably the greatest difficulty confronting the theatre of fact—when it remains fact—the matter of motives.

The subcommittee chairman lays the responsibility for what befell the Pueblo largely at the door of the military bureaucracy:

> It is the unanimous view of this subcommittee that there exist serious deficiencies in the organizational and administrative military command structure of both the Department of the Navy and the Department of Defense. The inquiry reveals the existence of a vast and complex military structure capable of acquiring almost infinite amounts of information but without a demonstrated ability to relay this information to those charged with the responsibility for making decisions.

The court of inquiry is less sympathetic. As Bucher reads a list of the members of his crew—"Children really. Kids"—to

113

whom he wishes to pay tribute, the verdicts are rendered on him and his men.

> SECRETARY OF THE NAVY: Commander Lloyd Mark Bucher should be court-martialled for five alleged offenses.
>
> BUCHER: What I did out there was the best possible military maneuver I could make at the time to accomplish the many things that had to be accomplished . . . namely . . . namely . . . the saving of life. . . .
>
> SECRETARY OF THE NAVY: I make no judgment concerning the guilt or innocence of these officers. It is my opinion, however, that they have suffered enough. The charges against all of the officers will be dismissed. Every effort is being made to correct any Navy deficiencies which may have contributed to Pueblo's seizure. The Navy leaders are determined that the lessons learned from this tragedy shall be translated into effective action.

Although Bucher responds that he believes in the United States "with all of my might," he also acknowledges that what has taken place was an experience he will have to think about "for a long time in order to come to a sensible conclusion. I'll never be able to understand it." He is left alone on a darkening stage, continuing to read the names of his crew.

He is scapegoat and flawed hero, the violator of one code in behalf of another, a figure who raises questions at the same time as he arouses sympathy. There exists the very real possibility that his ship indeed did violate North Korean territorial waters— a possibility *Pueblo* almost inexplicably does not explore. Inexplicably, that is, in terms of the political realities of the situation. In terms of the purely human realities, which are Greenberg's primary concern, the reasons for the failure are obvious: a *guilty* hero or victim-figure is far less likely to enlist our response. Yet, given the testimony of Bucher's executive officer, it is altogether likely that the Pueblo, with its faulty navigational system, may have been inside the twelve-mile limit sanctified by a UN Law of the Sea Conference in 1958. Exercising his right of selection, Greenberg in a sense exercises the right to ignore a question of right and wrong, of truth and duplicity.

This suggests one of the reasons the play, and much of the theatre of fact, is ultimately unsatisfactory. It adds no new dimension, no new insight, to the newspaper accounts. Its sympathy for Bucher—a sympathy it is difficult not to share—is clear; its presentation is in accord with the public record. It documents the fact that the commander was in a perhaps impossible situation—a probably unnecessary situation—and that he reacted as a human being whose acts were governed by his own concept of necessity and of the human realities of the moment. It offers a man who loves his country, who is a patriot, but who *does* give up the ship; an officer and a man acting in what he conceived to be the best interests of his men. What it does not offer is a more than surface exploration of the essential questions raised by the way the government acted—of why, for instance, Bucher could be judged wrong in what *he* did and the government, by its own lights, right in its later simultaneous confession and repudiation of that confession in order finally to free the crew—or of the depths of the moral issues involved.

In purely theatrical terms, Greenberg fails to dramatize his material as effectively as he might have. The play loses much of its potential impact by a blurring of the characters into what becomes "the crew," not individuals. Then, too, Bucher's closeness, even paternalism, to his crew and the full drama of their capture on the high seas—both clearly evident in *Bucher: My Story*—are only erratically present. It is almost as if Greenberg's fidelity to the known "facts" had blinded him to their very real, very intense, dramatic potential. It does not entirely cripple the play; it does, however, lessen its impact and its resonance. More than this, it suggests that the theatre of fact can go only so far before a transforming act of creativity—not necessarily a fictionalizing—is needed to reveal the full implications *of* the facts. *Pueblo* never achieves that transformation; it only points toward its possibility.

*What sort of villains would we
be, if we did, for our own
benefit, the things we do for
our country?*

Soldiers

Initially banned in London, but eventually produced even there,
Rolf Hochhuth's *Soldiers* stirred nearly as much controversy in
some quarters as his earlier condemnation of Pope Pius XII in
The Deputy. It was easy to see why—provided you were British,
but more difficult otherwise.

Soldiers is in many ways superior to *The Deputy* (which is far
from saying it is a really good play). But, like the latter, it is
unlikely ever to be discussed primarily in those terms. For better or worse, Hochhuth has a way of making "technique" seem
somewhat irrelevant. Whether or not one happens to agree with
him, his concerns are a far cry from the soporific concerns of
Broadway and his seriousness as an involved, even a tortured,
participant in the life of his time is beyond dispute.

In *Soldiers* Hochhuth comes to grips with one of the greatest
figures of our time as he confronts two of the most overriding
questions of that time. The man is Winston Churchill; the
questions, the morality of saturation bombing of civilian population centers and the extent to which the demands of war or
other political necessities justify acts that, in the normal course
of things, would be termed immoral. Both in their specifics and
in extension they have as much relevance today as they did at
the time *Soldiers* supposedly takes place.

117

Hochhuth employs the long-since trite device of a play within a play or, more accurately, a play within a rehearsal. It is, in this case, quite unnecessary and artificial but, that said, one nonetheless can see the reasons for it. The time is autumn, 1964, the centenary of the first Geneva Convention, and, as Hochhuth notes in the published version, "ten years since the explosion of the first hydrogen bomb relegated America's membership in the International Red Cross to the realm of black humor."

A group of actors is beginning a dress rehearsal of *The Little London Theatre of the World* (derived from Calderón's *El gran teatro del mundo*) amid the ruins of St. Michael's Cathedral in Coventry, destroyed by German bombers in November, 1940. Dorland is a theatrical director about to die (his name is from the probable author of the first *Everyman*). He has written a play with which he hopes to atone for his role in the bombing of German cities during World War II and to awaken both his own generation and that of his RAF-pilot son to the fact that the Red Cross Convention on the protection of cities from aerial warfare should become international law. "Everyman . . . has become a soldier," Hochhuth writes. "In an age of general conscription and the use of bombs and rockets primarily against the defenseless, a man's conscience is exposed to its most violent ordeals during his years of military service."

Within this framework, a series of characters who are on hand for the next day's centenary observation wander across the stage: a judge, Dorland's son, a colonel in the West German Air Force (the swastika removed from his wartime medals), a Japanese professor mutilated at Nagasaki, a French general, and later, an American colonel and a Russian military attaché. "Try yourself to hit a tank—with a rocket," the Frenchman recommends. "Tanks move, towns stand still."

When they have passed, Dorland reminisces about a woman he had first encountered on the streets of Dresden when he was forced to bail out during a bombing raid. He reflects that

> on the second attack on Dresden, there happened to me something which seldom happens to us today, and which tomorrow will, for the men who fire the rockets, simply not be possible. I had to see, to *touch*

118

what I had killed. . . . This woman sat there, where the heat had thrown her down, the blast of the fire-storm all around her—eyes and flesh melted away, only the bridge of the nose, inexplicably, still covered with skin, as if fireproofed. And her hair had been preserved.

Tortured by his memories, he challenges his son: "A soldier is a man who fights other soldiers; a pilot, who aims at tanks, bridges, factories, dams. That is not you—as it was not me over Dresden."

The prologue to *Soldiers* is prolix almost to the point of self-indulgence. When Dorland remarks, "The theatre isn't a museum. History only ceases to be academic when it can illustrate for *us* and *now* man's inhumanity to man—the historical cliché," one feels inclined to wish Hochhuth would suspend the dramatized lecture and get on with a bit of the illustrating. When he does, the play, which is perhaps more effective on the printed page than on stage, achieves some moments of moving intensity and power.

Hochhuth takes as an epigraph lines from *Don Quixote*: "This belongs among those things which should not be investigated to the very end." As was widely publicized at the time, the British Lord Chamberlain, as well as the board of the British National Theatre, seemed to agree. Since Churchill is not presented as a villain (even, for that matter, if he were), it all seemed more than a trifle unnecessary.

Here, as was not the case with his depiction of Pius XII, Hochhuth permits Churchill the integrity of his motives, though he strongly questions the reasoning and consequences attendant upon them. He renders the prime minister as a blend of the heroic and the tragic (tragic in the Hegelian sense that both parties to the conflict must be right). Tragic, then, because of the rightness of his intentions in placing the interests of humanity above those of a quixotically, if not diabolically led, nation and because the innocent civilians who died in the firestorms of Hamburg and other cities possessed a *right* to live. And, he suggests, tragic also because the Poles, who provide the second theme of the play, were right in their demand for

119

justice, while Churchill, on a quite different level, was right in acquiescing to Stalin's demands.

In an interview with Martin Esslin, Hochhuth observed: "I don't agree with those dramatists like Dürrenmatt who proclaim the end of tragedy on the grounds that the day of the individual is past forever, that nobody is responsible any more. Those people forget one thing: the number of individuals who *did* achieve something has always been very, very small, throughout history."

The time of the play proper is April-July, 1943. Churchill, together with the British chief-of-staff, Sir Alan Brooke, and Churchill's long-time friend and adviser Lord Cherwell, is on the deck of the battleship H.M.S. *Duke of York*, bound for Scapa Flow. Lord Cherwell has conceived a formula for firestorms that will level the industrial quarters of all German cities of over 50,000 inhabitants. Of Cherwell, C. P. Snow has noted: "He was altogether a bit bigger than life-size." Hochhuth is less gentle, terming him "the Grand Cremator" and having him describe himself as the "torchbearer of saturation bombing." If *Soldiers* has a "villain," it is he. "Fire is *the* element of our age," he contends; "this war is to be won with fire." He and Brooke argue:

BROOKE: How is the fire in the cities to paralyze industry? . . .

CHERWELL: Krupp is right inside Essen. There are aircraft, tank and locomotive factories not far from the center of Kassel. It is not unusual. . . .

BROOKE: Quite, quite: where that is so, you must demolish the towns. But using aiming points.

CHERWELL: No, no, Sir Alan, set the place on *fire*: the dislocation of the working population, the gas, light and main water—*these* will paralyze industry. . . . The panicking force of fire is immeasurable.

In the absence of agreement from the field marshal, Churchill is more pragmatic: "Let me justify Gomorrah [codeword for the operation] politically: to render a million Germans home-

120

less—that is a victory; to puncture half a dozen oil tanks—that is not." He gives the order. Cherwell, with mounting fervor, and sketching with colored chalk, shows Churchill how the man-made firestorms are to be produced, creating "a single confla-gration . . . the burning inner city" in which air streams draw everything "centripetally toward the furnace." Churchill is almost awed. Regardless of his ultimate attitude, the viewer already is almost sickened, as much by the icy certainty and inhumanity of Cherwell as by the horror he describes.

Hochhuth's concurrent plot concerning what he alleges was the British responsibility for the death of the Polish prime minister in exile, General Sikorski, is, at least from a British point of view, more controversial. At the time *Soldiers* takes place, Churchill is under increasing pressure from Stalin to take a more active role in the European sector. He tells the Soviet ambassador: "The bombers *are* the Second Front." Then, too, the Polish exiles in London have contended that it was the Russians, not the Germans, who were responsible for the recent-ly discovered murder of four thousand Polish officers found in mass graves in Katyn, their hands tied behind their backs. Understandably, if perhaps not justifiably indignant, Stalin has recommended that Churchill both "make certain substitutions in the membership of the Polish Government" and agree to extensive Soviet annexation of Polish territory. Brooke, cast as devil's advocate throughout, demands:

> Is the Prime Minister of England to depose the Prime Minister of Poland? . . . What are we *not* doing for Stalin as it is? . . .

> CHURCHILL: What is the Kremlin not doing for *us*? [Stalin] is taking at least a hundred and ninety German divisions off our backs, while we—how many is it, Brookie, that we are driving back in the desert?

> BROOKE: Fifteen, or thereabouts.

Thus, although he has genuine affection and respect for Sikorski, Churchill's bargaining position is extremely weak. "Our . . . breaches of contract quite entitle Stalin to make a

121

separate peace with Hitler," he admits. He is confronted with the need to placate Stalin by not permitting the investigation of the Katyn massacre the Poles are demanding. "The murders at Katyn lie in the past," he tells Sikorski, "and—to quote Stalin—the past belongs to God." The Polish leader is outraged:

> Four thousand of Poland's fourteen thousand officers have been found there, the elite of my officers . . . and is the Prime Minister of Poland to be forbidden even to *inquire* who the murderer is?
>
> CHURCHILL: But since you *know*—for *Poland's* sake do not ask *now*! . . . Do you want to write history? Then seek the truth. Or do you want to make it? Then it is facts that count. The dead are impartial, the dead have time to wait.
>
> SIKORSKI: Prime Minister—if the butchering of our officers is ever to make sense objectively—
>
> CHURCHILL: There is no objectivity in war. There is only an objective.
>
> SIKORSKI: The objective of our investigation is morally to force the butcher to restore, by treaty, the eastern half of Poland.
>
> CHURCHILL: *Morally*—force Stalin *morally*?

Because he does admire Sikorski and because he fears what Stalin's withdrawal from the war would mean, Churchill pleads with the general: "Stalin's demands are reasonable. All he demands from Germany is Königsberg. All he demands from Poland are the provinces she took from Russia—twenty years ago. Give up Lvov—for Breslau." But the line already has been drawn—between the patriot-idealist and the political realist, between the nation that is helpless and the nation that is strong. When Sikorski announces that his ambassadors already have demanded an International Red Cross investigation of the graves at Katyn, Churchill feels called upon to thwart him. When he tries to exact Churchill's promise that the Russian-Polish frontiers will not be discussed prior to the defeat of Germany, Churchill reminds him that no English, American, or Polish soldier has even reached the continent. "Why should Stalin let us tie his hands regarding European frontier solutions," he asks, "since, from his point of view, we are not even fighting a European war at all?"

In Act 2, subtitled "The Bed" for the simple reason that Churchill spends almost its entire duration in one, the prime minister receives a cable indicating that Stalin has broken relations with Poland. Cherwell comments: "Now, finally, overboard with that Pole." And, a bit later, quoting Napoleon: "A patriot who has lost his country must lose his life."

Although it is never explicitly stated, *Soldiers* strongly suggests that Sikorski's death in a plane crash shortly thereafter was engineered by British Intelligence. Though unable to produce documentation to substantiate this accusation, Hochhuth contends that he himself has seen the proof, documents now in the vault of a Swiss bank and not to be available for fifty years. But in an interview in the German newspaper *Die Zeit*, he comments: "I am convinced that if Churchill is responsible, it is because he had no choice. In 1943, if the Polish exile regime under Sikorski had continued to provoke the Kremlin as it had done until then, the danger of Stalin's leaving the war would have arisen. What would the Western Powers have done? They were not capable of bringing off a landing in France."

Churchill learns of Sikorski's death while he is in the garden of the prime minister's residence at Chequers, where he is being confronted with Bishop Bell of Chichester's plea against the bombing of cities.

BELL: Do you not shrink from actions which are called murder when Hitler performs them?

CHURCHILL: [The bombing is] unavoidable: adversaries in war will use each other's methods and worse besides, each other's qualities. . . . One must be silent about many things that one has done in war.

Thus Hochhuth raises again the perennial question, evident in the careers of figures as diverse as Richelieu and Lenin: can there be a distinction between public and private morality, between the political and the personal act? It is explicit in

Churchill's observation, "Men may be bound by friendship, nations only by interest: a discovery which makes the greater man the lesser human being," and even more in Dorland's quotation from a Churchill essay on Asquith: "What sort of villains would we be, if we did, for our own benefit, the things we do for our country?"

For Hochhuth, then, there is no question of casting Churchill in the role of villain. A character asserts, "The Prime Minister is a great man, and that in nature is something terrible." Dorland is asked by his son whether Churchill was responsible for Sikorski's death. He replies: "If he thought it necessary, yes. If not, no. . . . Without a doubt he thought it necessary to save the alliance that saved the world."

Whatever one may think of Hochhuth as a playwright, it would be impossible not to acknowledge that he has employed the theatre as an arena in which the great moral issues of our time can be raised. In the interview cited earlier, he suggested: "If you read the third act of my play you will notice that there is something like a religious viewpoint in it, in the widest possible sense. . . . This is what interests me, why there should be wars, why people should rush to their perdition. . . . One must strive to achieve a real improvement in the world. But I must confess that I am deeply pessimistic about the feasibility of such improvements. But that does not mean one should not try."

If that is the playwright's obligation—and it would certainly seem to be one aspect of it—perhaps it is the audience's to react, not with outrage at the challenge to myths (or realities) long considered inviolable, but with concern at questions that seemingly have no answers but someday must find them.

PART THREE:
OTHER CONTROVERSIES

A deputy of Christ
who sees these things and
nonetheless
permits reasons
of state to seal his lips—
who wastes
even one day in thought...
that Pope is ... a criminal.

The Deputy

The Deputy has been called the most controversial play of our time. In the foreword to an anthology of the reviews and essays Rolf Hochhuth's play evoked, Eric Bentley went even further, describing the reaction to the play as "almost certainly the largest storm ever raised by a play in the whole history of the drama." The reason is as obvious as the response was emotional: politicians and potentates, heroes and saints—figures from virtually every walk of life and every century—have been scorned, vilified, and condemned by playwrights. No one, however, could remember a dramatist ever taking on a pope, at least not a pope only recently dead—one, moreover, considered by many to be a saint—and indicting him for opportunism, moral cowardice, and hypocrisy at a time when a few words from him might have saved the lives of millions. And so, although it somehow appalled one to see rosary-bearing, placard-carrying protesters parading outside a Broadway theatre, it required little effort to realize the sense of outrage they felt. Whether validly or otherwise, Hochhuth had not merely offended their sensi-

127

bilities, but challenged their certainties. Challenging certainties can be a provocative, even a dangerous game.

Any discussion of *The Deputy* has to proceed from the fact that there was no stage at which it was possible to criticize the play fairly on the basis of its productions (least of all its New York production, which fell little short of butchery), if only because of its length. It would have required some seven hours to perform in full. What follows, then, is based exclusively on the published version, with its extensive "Sidelights on History" and its detailed, often ironically funny stage directions. Although the inclusion of such historical "documentation" may make it sound like a work that merits consideration exclusively as a polemic, not as a play, that is not the case. It has weaknesses and strengths in both areas, but an absence of "theatricality" is not one of them.

Hochhuth's theme is clear and hammered home in scene after scene: Pius XII, with an enormous bank of moral and spiritual credit to draw upon, should have condemned the Nazi atrocities against the Jews. Not to do so was to default not only on his role as the Vicar—the Deputy—of Christ on earth and leader of the most unified religious force in the world, but also on his role as a human being in a position to save other human beings at a time when he alone might have affected their fate. Pius "spoke," Hochhuth acknowledges, but in words that were so deliberately generalized, so hollow and equivocal, that Hitler felt no need to listen. He said nicely, in the carefully couched, fussily diplomatic pronunciamentos at which he was skilled, what should have been said in terms that would stir moral and emotional indignation. So doing, he abdicated on his responsibility and must share in the guilt for the six million deaths that flowed from the "Final Solution."

The Deputy opens in the reception room of the papal legation in Berlin. It is August, 1942, and the sixty-nine-year-old nuncio, His Excellency Cesare Orsenigo, is alerting his newly appointed aide, a twenty-seven-year-old Jesuit priest named Riccardo Fontana, to the niceties of the ecclesio-political scene in wartime Germany. The nuncio is an historical figure, one of only five in the play; Riccardo is fictional, though much of his behavior is patterned on that of Provost Bernhard Lichtenberg

128

of Berlin Cathedral, who prayed publicly for the Jews and in time asked to be permitted to share their fate in the East.

If there is anything for Orsenigo to take consolation from in these dark and uncertain times, it is "how eagerly both sides are courting us." Both Allies and Axis recognize the unimportance of Stalin's classic question: "How many divisions has the pope?" and accept Churchill's reply: "A number of legions not always visible on parade."

It is the sudden appearance of Kurt Gerstein, a lieutenant in the Waffen-SS, that brings the play into focus. Gerstein himself is one of the more intriguing of World War II figures. He had been active as a youth leader with the Evangelical Church and wrote and distributed anti-Nazi pamphlets for the Confessional Church until he was arrested in 1936. When he was released, he joined the SS and thereafter led a double life while he determined the accuracy of the rumors concerning the genocide of the Jews. By 1942 he was "driven without respite" to make what he had seen known to church leaders.

Gerstein bursts into the reception room, determined to get a message to the Vatican. He has just come from Poland—from Belzec and Treblinka—where he has seen the atrocities at first hand. The nuncio is reluctant to hear a confirmation of crimes he cannot help but be aware of. He wishes to continue to deal with the Nazis in the "calm spirit and friendly manner" the state secretary in the German foreign office found so welcome. He tries not to listen, insisting he has no authority to interfere.

> GERSTEIN: Authority! Here in Berlin you represent
> the—the Deputy of Christ,
> and you can close your eyes to the worst horror
> that man has ever inflicted upon man.
> You hold your peace while every hour . . .

The nuncio attempts to terminate the discussion. But Gerstein will not be calmed: "I know very well, Your Excellency—you can't do anything./ But the Holy Father must take action,/ must speak for the world's conscience." How, he demands, can the Vatican continue to be a party to the Concordat with Hitler? How long can it continue to espouse "peace with

129

murderers"? The nuncio is moved—but not far enough. Whatever his own feelings on the matter, he tells Gerstein, he "cannot simply take account of them." He has attempted to intervene in private, but his position requires that he avoid involvement in "any cause of conflict between Rome and your authorities." When he starts to leave, Gerstein reminds him:

> That blood guilt,
> Excellency, falls upon us all
> if we keep silent!

If the nuncio will not act, Riccardo will. For practical purposes, his course is already set. Before he leaves the room with Orsenigo, he tells Gerstein, "I will find you."

In his meticulously researched *German Catholics and Hitler's Wars*, the American sociologist Gordon Zahn has written:

> Considerations of prudence and a regard for the benefits to be gained through continued diplomatic contact argued against punitive action on the part of the Holy See; yet, in effect, as long as papal recognition continued, the German Catholic was in the difficult position of being morally obliged to render obedience to a presumably legitimate authority dedicated to the destruction of the moral values represented by his Church.

For Riccardo, there will be no "considerations of prudence." A scene in the cellar of the Jägerskellar in Falkensee, near Berlin, shows a party presided over by Adolf Eichmann and attended by various military, industrial, and scientific figures, among them The Doctor, who "has the stature of Absolute Evil." Following this, Riccardo appears at Gerstein's apartment. It is the next morning and he is not the only other person there. Gerstein has been hiding a Jew named Jacobson from the authorities. When Riccardo arrives, he assures Gerstein that he has "the honor to know the Pope well," and insists: "I give my *guarantee*, Herr Gerstein,/ His Holiness will make a protest." Gerstein tells him:

No need for you to tell Rome anything that's *new*.
Only arouse a sense of outrage.
Those who keep silence are accessories to murder,
and they imperil their immortal souls.

Riccardo has complete, almost arrogant, confidence that the
pope will protest. To him, there seems no other possibility.
Gerstein feels differently, but he accepts the priest's personal
sincerity. He will, however, put him to the test. He asks him for
his cassock and passport so that Jacobson can cross the Brenner
Pass. Although initially reluctant, Riccardo gives them to him.
In exchange he receives not just Jacobson's own passport, with
its large *J*, but the yellow star he has been forced to wear.

Returning to Rome, in February, 1943, Riccardo quickly
attempts to follow through on his guarantee to Gerstein. His
father is one of the highest-ranking laymen at the Vatican and
he seeks to dissuade him. But Riccardo implores:

Let us admit at last:
these flames are also *our* trial by fire!
Who will, in times to come, respect us still
as moral arbiters if, in *this* time,
we fail so miserably?

The senior Fontana tries to reason with him, to remind him
that although the pope has not issued the denunciation he
demands—the protest that would "stir the world to pity, to
outrage and to action"—"his heart is with the victims." He will
protest against Hitler's atrocities when the time comes that it no
longer will imperil the Church. But it is the pope's voice, not his
heart, Riccardo is concerned about. His father tries to convince
him that in Pius's view only Hitler has the power "to save all
Europe from the Russians," that, moreover, a protest "would
be without effect, or place/ the Church in Germany in grave
jeopardy."

At the height of their argument they are joined by Fontana's
good friend The Cardinal, a diplomat who at first sight "looks
like a clubwoman." The cardinal is symptomatic of one of the
recurring weaknesses in Hochhuth's play. In his attitude toward

Riccardo's anguish, he glories in reasons of state, employing them as the "rational" man that he is. In his person he is a caricature, a rotund and jovial gossip who is too intelligent ever to show himself in any way superior to the "Chief," as he calls the pope. In one sense, however, he minces no words: "The Chief will not expose himself to danger for the Jews." He can, of course, rationalize it away to the last comma. Besides, he wants to know:

> Can *you* guarantee that threats
> will *really not* aggravate the situation?

> RICCARDO: Your Eminence, a hundred thousand Jew-
> ish families in Europe
> face certain murder!
> It could not, could not, possibly be *worse*!

By now, Riccardo's father is on his side, though he attempts to appease the cardinal out of his fear that Riccardo's tone will prevent others from listening to him. "You are right, my boy," he tells him when the cardinal has gone, "but you have no say."

When we next see Riccardo, it is October, 1943, and the situation has, if anything, worsened. Now, the deportations of the Jews are taking place, as the German ambassador stated, "as it were, under the Pope's windows." Still, Pius has not spoken, not even when, as Gerald Reitlinger puts it in *The Final Solution*, Jews were being "herded to their death from the very shadow of St. Peter's." As Hochhuth acknowledges, many of Rome's churches and monasteries were concealing Jews and the pope had helped to pay ransom to the Nazis to save still others. It is in one of the monasteries, at a time when the cardinal is also on hand, that Riccardo and Gerstein next turn up. By now, even the cardinal thinks the pope will have to denounce the Nazis. He tells Gerstein that the Germans have taken one step too many in "that business with the Jews."

Riccardo is not so certain. "Suppose the Pope does what he always does," he suggests, "I mean, does nothing." What will they do then? Riccardo knows what *he* can do, he can go with the victims. It may not save a single Jew—indeed, it is almost

132

certain not to—but perhaps it may save the Church. He will be the Deputy, the deputy for the Deputy of Christ:

> You must see that the silence of the Pope
> in favor of the murderers imposes
> a guilt upon the Church for which we must atone.
> And since the Pope, although only a man,
> can actually represent God on earth,
> I . . . a poor priest . . . if need be
> can also represent the Pope—*there*
> where the Pope ought to be standing today.

When finally, in Act 4, the pope appears for the first time, Riccardo's worst fears are confirmed. Not coincidentally, so are the worst flaws of *The Deputy*. Pius comes on, "much less a person than an institution," Hochhuth notes, and his first words, spoken to Count Fontana, immediately violate credibility: "We are filled with burning concern for Italy's factories./ Power plants, railroad terminals, dams, indeed every enterprise/ stands in imperative need of protection."

They go on to talk about securities and about the fact that they are unable to see the financial records of the Jesuits. When the subject of the Jews in Rome finally comes up, the pope finds the actions of the Germans "tactless . . . extremely bad behavior." When, however, the count asks him to have forbearance toward his son because Riccardo has seen the Jewish children thrown onto the trucks in Berlin, the pope unleashes an angry rejoinder in which he insists that "whoever wants to help must not provoke Hitler." He mentions the hundreds of Jews they have hidden and the thousands of passports they have issued. Besides, he insists, the Germans ignored his last Christmas message, "one single plea for brotherly love." Realizing that Riccardo's passion will accomplish nothing, the count asks the pope if he may speak in his stead:

> Your Holiness, may I ask in all humility:
> Warn Hitler that you will *compel*
> five hundred million Catholics to

133

make Christian protest
if he goes on with these mass killings!

Instead, the pope responds that disaster looms for all of Christian Europe unless "God makes Us, the Holy See, the *mediator.*" Although the terror against the Jews is "loathsome," Germany must remain viable to "hold the frontiers against the East." He will, however, issue a proclamation: "No one shall say/ We sacrificed the law of Christian love/ to political calculations—no!" He will not, however, mention the Jews specifically, he must "continue to shelter the spirit of *neutrality.*" Midway through dictating to the scribe, he suddenly digresses to talk to Count Fontana about the Vatican's Hungarian railroad securities and the need to protect their investments. That, Hochhuth suggests, is vastly more important to the pontiff than the plight of the Jews.

When Fontana contends that the pope's statement "cannot be construed as a reference to the Jewish problem," the papal patience is exhausted. Has he not spoken "of men *of all races*" in voicing his concern for the "aggravated sufferings" brought on by the war? Fontana makes one final plea that the pope send Hitler an ultimatum. When it is ignored, Riccardo attaches the yellow Star of David to his cassock. The pope is "struck dumb," and in signing his proclamation drops the pen and smears ink on his fingers. The scribe goes out to get a basin and, after he returns, Riccardo speaks his final words to the pope: "God shall not destroy His Church/ only because a Pope shrinks from His summons."

When Riccardo leaves, the pope sits down and begins to wash his hands—Hochhuth's New Pilate—for a moment stunned to speechlessness. Recovering, he insists, "Whatever *has been granted Us to do was done.*"

All that comes after is in a sense anticlimactic. In Auschwitz, where he has gone with the Jews, Riccardo encounters The Doctor, a figure based partially on the infamous Doctor Mengele, but in Hochhuth's eyes more an "uncanny visitant from another world," the Devil, who describes himself as "lord of life and death in this place." He tells Riccardo that he will be his private chaplain. If he insists on being gassed instead, The

Doctor asserts, he will "die as the heroes of today do die, namelessly,/ snuffed out by powers they have never known,/ let alone can fight. In other words, meaninglessly." Why has he done what he has, Riccardo asks? "To challenge the Old Gent,/ to provoke him so limitlessly/ that He would have to give answer./ Even if only the negative answer/ which can be His sole excuse, as/ Stendhal put it: that He doesn't exist."

It is that he wishes to show to Riccardo, that he wants to convince him of. As the play nears its end, it appears he may have succeeded:

> For the past week
> I have been burning the dead ten hours a day.
> And with every human body that I burn
> a portion of my faith burns also.
> God burns.
> Corpses—a conveyor belt of corpses.
> History is a highway paved with carrion . . .
> If I knew that He looks on—
> I would have to—hate Him.

When Gerstein, who has come in an attempt to rescue Riccardo, replies that "none of us understands Him any longer," Riccardo can only say in anguish: "I am—I would be frightened of rescue/ by Him . . . The Monster that devours its young."

Although he is frightened of what is to come, Riccardo insists that Jacobson, who also has turned up in Auschwitz, use the documents Gerstein has brought. It is not to be. The Doctor knows both of them and, as the play ends, Riccardo has been shot by an SS man as he attempted to shoot The Doctor. Both he and Jacobson are on the way to the crematorium. Like the six million jews, Riccardo has been "abandoned by everyone, abandoned even by the Deputy of Christ."

Hochhuth is hardly alone in taking the stance that Pius XII, having failed to condemn unequivocally the Nazi extermination of the Jews, merits not simply condemnation but damnation. His position has yet to be effectively refuted. In a sense, perhaps, it cannot be. There have, however, been numerous attempts, and it repeatedly has been pointed out that Rabbi

135

Zolli, the sixty-five-year-old Rabbi of Rome, who was baptized a Catholic in 1945, took as his baptismal name "Eugenio Maria" in honor of the pope (Eugenio Pacelli), "for interceding on behalf of the Jews during the occupation."

Almost inexplicably, Pius did not speak; it is a fact and a completely valid subject for drama. The problem of *The Deputy* lies elsewhere—in Hochhuth's failure to acknowledge the moral complexities involved, his willingness to present his characters as not merely indifferent but altogether unaware of the human and spiritual dimensions of the question. Pius may have been precisely the cold and prissily unfeeling businessman-diplomat that Hochhuth presents. But to make him superficial, to exaggerate his concern with finances, the supposed menace posed by "the Russian colossus," and the necessity of his own role as mediator to a point bordering on caricature is unconvincing not only historically but dramatically.

One of the curiosities of *The Deputy* is that Hochhuth seems simply not to care about the inner workings of his "villain," about the *why* of his action. Nor, oddly, does he seem notably more interested in the motivations of most of the others. They are viewed almost exclusively in the light of their attitude toward the pope, on the one hand, and as one-dimensional automatons on the other. Having decided there was no room for uncertainty, that it simply was not possible, Hochhuth will not permit it in his characters either.

It is revealing that the stage directions read: "At first His Holiness appears only as an intense white gleam." "White gleams" simply won't do; they cannot provide theatrical antagonists any more than they can provide dramatic characters. If Hochhuth's Pius is to be held accountable *as a human being* for his failure to act, if he is to be accepted as something other than a scapegoat for the failure of Germany, the Church, and the West to respond in the face of the most incomprehensible evil in history, then he must be seen to *be* a human being, not a collection of attitudes and surface details drawn from a newspaper morgue, one who "strikes the pose in which he likes to be photographed" and makes the same "grand gestures" in private as on the balcony overlooking St. Peter's Square. If he is to be damned for his decision not to speak, it should at least be shown that his character possessed sufficient dimension for there to have been a question and a decision. It is a failure of creative imagination, not of historical research, that largely invalidates him as a character.

The motives the pope is given—financial greed, *realpolitik*, anti-Communist fanaticism, anti-Semitism, cowardice, an excessive concern with the allegiance of German Catholics—completely preclude the possibility that his decision, wrong though it very probably was, might conceivably have been made in good faith. Is it just possible that the pope *did* believe, as his close associate Cardinal Montini (later Pope Paul VI) insisted, that "an attitude of protest and condemnation . . . would have been not only futile but harmful: that is the long and the short of the matter"? It is a hypothetical question, of course, and one that very likely never can be answered, but to suggest that it was *not* a question is not borne out by the facts in some, more localized, actions on the part of the hierarchy.

If it is difficult to believe that the pope was right, it is equally difficult not to believe that he thought, or had convinced himself, that he *was* right; that it was purely a question of deliberate obfuscation when he pleaded for those who, because of their *stirps* ("race") "are condemned to death or exposed to progressive misery." It is one thing to question his judgment, another to presume to *know* his motives.

It can, of course, be argued that Pius XII and Riccardo, like Gerstein and The Doctor, are intended not as characters but as figures in a modern morality, vehicles for moral outrage and compassion on the one hand and inhumanity and evil on the other. But to suggest, as one Swiss critic did, that Hochhuth "does not have to understand" his character "because he does not have to forgive" him is hardly valid. Perhaps he does not have to forgive him—forgiveness is something beyond a human prerogative—but given the nature of the play, he does have to convince the audience. And to achieve this, it is more effective to acknowledge that there were areas of uncertainty and to respond to them than it is to deny their possibility.

What one most longs to see in *The Deputy* is any indication of the figure who, according to an aide to the German ambassador at the Vatican, Albrecht von Kessel, "struggled, I know, day after day, week after week, month after month, to find an answer."

If, in the end, *The Deputy* still manages to move us, to be one of the most significant dramatic works produced in the 60s, it is despite its essentially simplistic characterization, failure to explore motivations, and the ponderousness of its free-verse form. It forces us to face once more the question of power and responsibility—and perhaps the question of Grace—and to face it in terms of an event that to this day almost defies the imagination. What is regrettable is that Hochhuth, though he employs it as an epigraph, did not elect to portray that question in terms of Revelation 3:16: "So, because you are lukewarm, and neither cold nor hot, I will spew you out of my mouth." The world of men, the world even of the Deputy of Christ, is more often than not a world of grays, a world of the "lukewarm." The figures in *The Deputy* are "cold" and "hot."

All of us
I want to make that very clear
did nothing but our duty

The Investigation

If Peter Weiss has ever heard that old saw, "If you have a message, call Western Union," he shows no sign of it. "Every word that I write for publication is political," he has said. "It is intended to make contact with large groups of people and to achieve a definite effect." Sometimes he succeeds, sometimes he fails. Nowhere does he make a more concentrated, more deeply committed effort than in *The Investigation*, his 1965 drama about the horrors and hypocrisy of Auschwitz, seen through the eyes of its victims and its perpetrators. *Vietnam Discourse*, *Trotsky in Exile*, and *The Song of the Lusitanian Bogey* are more overtly political, perhaps more angry; *The Investigation*, despite its documentary form, is more personal. Weiss may abhor the American war in Indochina, may find unjustifiable the Soviet treatment of Trotsky, may consider intolerable the Portuguese suppression of the 1961 uprising in Angola, but it is the events of Auschwitz that he feels.

In the 1965 essay *My Place*, he writes of Auschwitz as "a place for which I was destined but which I managed to avoid. . . . I have no relation to it, except that my name was on the lists of the people who were supposed to be sent there forever." He has "had no experience of this place," but he so easily might have. Born in 1916, in Nowawes near Berlin, the son of a prosperous textile manufacturer (a Czech Jew who

139

converted to Christianity) and a Swiss mother, he almost from the first knew what it was to be apart, "a stranger wherever I went." He emigrated with his family in 1934, first to England, then to Czechoslovakia, Switzerland, and in 1939, to Sweden, where he lives today. He thus escaped the physical fact of Auschwitz, though not its intellectual and emotional impact. Its reality, still almost incomprehensible despite the millions of words, the thousands of photographs, the almost countless works of fiction and nonfiction that have been devoted to it, was what he wanted to convey in *The Investigation*.

Weiss has said that he wanted a "scientific investigation" of that reality, and for it he drew upon the testimony of hundreds of witnesses at the 1964 Frankfurt war crimes trial and the extraordinary reports of Bernd Naumann in the *Frankfurter Allgemeine Zeitung*. The result, in eleven cantos or blocks, is more intellectually overwhelming than it is dramatically moving or effective. Having cast himself as the observer, the transmitter of accounts, Weiss goes one step further: he insists that the witnesses "become mere speaking tubes," nine representatives of the hundreds who actually appeared. The logic of the decision is clear; the effect is problematic.

Weiss is, of course, right in referring to "the impossibility of actually staging the events, of having people 'act' the concentration camp," and the sense of horror we experience in any coming to grips with those events is present in *The Investigation*. Whether the play takes that sense of horror, that attempt to comprehend, a step further is the question that must be asked—the demand that must be made.

Of the anonymous witnesses, two worked with the camp administration; the remainder—two of them women—were among the surviving prisoners. The eighteen accused are specific figures, their names taken from the trial records. But, says Weiss in a note to the published version, their real existence is as "symbols of a system that implicated in its guilt many others who never appeared in court."

In the first of the cantos (called "songs" in the English edition), the camp functionaries tell of the "mechanics" of Auschwitz: how the trains arrived, how the prisoners were received, and the prisoners of the selection process, that act in which man played God, the doctor gesturing right or left from the platform and with that gesture dealing life, at least for a time, or death in the gas chambers and crematoria:

> The officer who divided us
> was very friendly
> I asked him
> where the others were going
> and he said
> they're just going to shower now
> You'll see them again in an hour

As will happen so often during the trial, there is an immediate denial, an insistence that the witness has confused the accused with someone else. The accused "never took part in the selections on the platform." Even those who, in time, admit to some minimal involvement participated on only a few occasions; they were substitutes, called upon accidentally or because the staff happened to be shorthanded. Always, of course, they acted only because of orders; they bore none of the responsibility, shared none of the guilt: "I only did my duty. . . . Anyway what could I do/ Orders are orders."

If the play has a leitmotiv, that is it: "I only did my duty." One of the accused, Dr. Lucas, is asked what he did on the platform. Denying *any* involvement with what occurred there, he tells of speaking to an archbishop who was a friend of his and to a prominent lawyer. He explains that he was told by both of them that, although illegal orders need not be obeyed, such an attitude "should not be carried to the extreme." They were, after all, at war and "all sorts of things were going on."

Succeeding cantos—"The Song of the Camp," "The Song of the Swing," "The Song of the Possibility of Survival"—tell of the processing and treatment of the prisoners, of the dehumanization and degradation that became an omnipresent factor in their lives:

> Only the cunning survived
> only those who every day
> with unrelenting alertness
> took and held their bit of ground

141

All others, those who were unfit, or slow, or gentle, or bewildered, or who mourned the dead and the dying, "were
crushed." To survive, it was necessary to become a special-duty
prisoner, to exploit one's skills or one's good fortune. With
sufficient cunning, says one prisoner-doctor, one could obtain
"practically anything." But for the others, the average prisoners, it was impossible to hold out for more than three months.
In any case, says another:

> The question
> of right and wrong
> didn't exist any longer
> The only thing that counted
> was what was immediately useful

As detail is piled upon detail—the medical experiments, the
sadism, the shootings, the bestiality, the wanton cruelty, the
types of confinement, the use of the camp labor by firms that
are today prosperous and respected—the effect becomes deaden-
ing, a recital of horrors that in repetition loses much of the
horror of the individual act. The sheer weight of the facts dulls
the senses. T. S. Eliot once observed that men cannot bear very
much reality. Nor can they bear too much shock without
becoming if not inured, perhaps insensitive. The death of one
child, flung against a wall by an SS man, the injection of one
prisoner with phenol, these are personal, something to which we
can relate and experience with personal pain—something we
can experience and something the playwright can convey. The
death of millions is beyond, at least almost beyond, our comprehension, beyond our ability to assimilate in other than
intellectual terms. Knowing the horror, we cease to know it.

But Weiss is concerned with something beyond the atrocities
perpetrated at Auschwitz. As a Marxist, he endeavors to show as
well "the role of German big industry in exterminating the
Jews. I want to brand Capitalism which even benefited from the
experiments of the gas chambers." He is concerned with the
culpability of a society and a system that he believes could, if
given the opportunity, display the same inhumanity in some
new and "far more efficient" guise. A witness insists:

142

> . . . If they had not been designated
> prisoners
> they could equally well have been guards
> We must drop the lofty view
> that the camp world
> is incomprehensible to us
> We all knew the society
> that produced a government
> capable of creating such camps

It is what the playwrights of the theatre of controversy say to us over and over again: we are all at least potentially guilty of the evils, the crimes, and sometimes merely the errors of judgment or failures of courage they indict. Whether it is in terms of the Hammarskjöld of *Murderous Angels*, the McCarthyism of *In the Matter of J. Robert Oppenheimer*, the racist murders of Auschwitz, or the immorality of Vietnam, silence is not golden; the meek do not inherit the earth only the aftereffects and the possibility that the *next* Hitler or McCarthy or Vietnam will be worse than the first. It is what the concluding witness of *The Investigation* tells the court:

> I . . . only wish to bring to mind
> that what they did
> could not have been carried out
> without the support
> of millions of others

And of yet more millions who merely looked away.

In attempting to de-emotionalize the issue, to simply *present* it in the confrontation of the witnesses and the accused and the questions and replies of the prosecution and the defense, Weiss declines to moralize. That he also declines to dramatize, save to the extent that the selection and arrangement constitute dramatization, cuts both ways. The witnesses and the accused give completely conflicting accounts and interpretations of the same events. Yet, there is no real conflict. The sheer weight of the evidence overwhelms it.

In failing to explore why the guards, the officers, the doctors,

143

acted as they did and, even more, in his deliberate decision to make his witnesses anonymous representatives rather than individuals, Weiss emerges with an account not a drama, which adds little to our knowledge and nothing to our comprehension. "You listen if you want to, and if you don't, you can shut your ears," Weiss said in an interview. "The play should be about four and a half hours long. . . . Part of the play's essential quality is its enormous length—it is unbearable. It should be unbearable."

But that is exactly what it is not. In the absence of characters who have an existence as individuals, its very repetition ultimately numbs rather than stirs the sensibilities. More than any play that I can think of, it confirms Max Frisch's contention that "the attempt to replace the theatrical vision through documents . . . will show us what the theatre cannot achieve." What it cannot achieve in the case of *The Investigation* is precisely what Weiss referred to in his account of his own visit to Auschwitz: "The living man who comes here, from another world, has nothing but his knowledge of figures, written reports, statements by witnesses; it lies heavy upon him, but he can only grasp what he experiences himself." Or, in the theatre, only what he sees embodied in the experiences of others. Others who are credible human beings, suffering an anguish and a torment that he hopes he will never have to share, an anguish and a torment that, if they are comprehensible at all, become so only in terms of the individuals who have been the victims and the victimizers. It is, in the end, a question of who and why and not of what.

*I'm not here to plead I took
orders. I had initiative. First
honest man who's stood in
your dock. Like you got the
Fuehrer himself in here.*

The Man in the Glass Booth

It is eight o'clock on a fine autumn morning and the Verdi
Requiem is playing in the background. "A bald-headed man in a
silk dressing-gown prays beside a tomb. A masterpiece rests
upon an easel. A glass elevator rises into one side of the room;
doors and a hallway lead off—one of the doors is locked."

The man is Arthur Goldman. He is fifty-two, a multimillion-
aire and real estate tycoon of olympian proportions, the friend
of senators, mayors—and, at least vicariously, it seems, of pro
football players. He is eccentric, quixotic at times, and seemingly secure in a world where flunkies do his every bidding and
New York financial circles cater to his whims. It is his birthday,
he is reminded by Charlie Cohn, his sycophantic secretary; it is
the twentieth of November, 1964. But it is—or will become—a
special day in his life for other reasons as well. They are very
much involved with that locked door mentioned in the stage
directions.

First, however, something else, something that perhaps plants
the seed that will lead Arthur Goldman from his comfortable world of concrete and glass towers, Rembrandts, Poussins,
1560 Tigerware jugs, Sunday afternoon football games, and

145

memories—or perhaps fantasies—of romping in the Pulitzer Fountain in front of the Plaza with Scott Fitzgerald, to a courtroom in Israel. Goldman learns of it in the morning paper as he half listens to Charlie read the copy for a new promotional brochure celebrating "his many brilliant ideas." "Jesus!" he cries. "The Pope's forgiven the Jews. Jesus. The Pope has forgiven the Jews." It evokes a curious reaction in him: on the one hand, a compulsion to identify people in terms of their Jewishness, on the other, an ironic anti-Semitism. It also prompts him to watch the pope on television. While he is doing so, his back is toward the elevator, which deposits a man of his own weight and age carrying a load of artificial flower plants. The man and Charlie take them off to the roof garden.

When they return, Goldman sees him, and the sight startles him. Goldman tells him he knows him, but in return receives only the comment "I've delivered here before." With that, the man leaves, only to return a moment later, ostensibly because he has left his hat behind. But Goldman knows—or thinks he knows—or pretends to think he knows—better. He tells Charlie to check up on the flower man, to have him followed. When the elevator returns yet again, he demands, "Who's this? My cousin again?" With that, he runs to the door and opens its various locks, and returns a moment later carrying a gun.

But it is only Dr. Kessel, come to give him an injection. The fact does not really divert his attention:

> You know that flower guy's name, Charlie? . . .
> That flower guy's name was Dorff, D-O-R-F-F.
> Dorff. Cousin Adolf, Charlie, Cousin Adolf
> Dorff.

Who is Dorff—really a cousin, a figure of his fantasies, a case of mistaken identity? Whoever he is, he prompts from Arthur Goldman one of what will be many illusive, seemingly unprovoked, and mystifying allusions to Adolf Hitler and his "Final Solution": "The Fuehrer said: 'In the Jewish people the will to self-sacrifice does not go beyond the individual's naked instinct for self-preservation.'" A moment later, he pushes a finger over his forehead to simulate a lock of hair and uses another to

146

effect a Hitlerian mustache: "Remember me." With that, he returns to the locked room, leaving Charlie and the doctor bewildered.

And they are not the only ones who are left bewildered. Robert Shaw's play, like his own novel on which it is based, is a compendium of deliberate—at times far too deliberate—attempts at obfuscation. What, for instance, of the mysterious locked room to which Goldman periodically repairs? What does it conceal? What of all these references to the Fuehrer? Are they simply the idiosyncrasies of an old man (in the novel, Goldman is seventy)? Quite early in the novel, though not in the play, Shaw suggests that they are something more: "Something concrete had begun to form in his brain. 'Perhaps it *was* all a mistake,' he said, with the sweetest of smiles." A page or two later, after he has briefly effected his Hitler pose and the doctor tells him he is not himself, he responds: "Perhaps will never be again. . . . The Pope's put me right on . . . you follow?"

Whatever the cause, Goldman from that morning becomes at least apparently schizoid, if not actually deranged, and so does the play. When the doctor suggests he is fevered, he denies it:

> Doc, I'm seeking both to inspire and distract myself. . . . From . . . the arbeit-macht-frei gray stone edifices . . . the innumerable three-floor-high-identical-edifices. Charlie, you call this a metropolis . . . that place . . . that place . . . was boundless. Being an athlete stood me in good stead. . . . It's not ended, you know. What can we do for the living?

He goes on to explain that the last time he saw Dorff, he was "goin'" from bed to bed, from litter to litter, from place to place . . . with his pistol. . . . Bang, bang, bang and I bring up the trolley."

Although he does not explicitly state it, Goldman obviously has been in a Nazi concentration camp. It does not accord with what the doctor and Charlie have known of him previously— but, then, what *have* they known of his past? Perhaps only that he joined his uncle's real estate firm sometime prior to 1947 and soon began to turn it into an ever-growing success. Like

147

Pinter, who directed the New York production of the play and in whose plays Shaw himself has appeared, Shaw is not given to filling in past histories or supplying fulsome biographies of his characters.

Goldman is, however, by now becoming increasingly obsessed with something in his past and with what it clearly has, on this particular morning, suggested to him about the present: "In Israel they can't even define it. J . . . E . . . W. . . . We're all Germans, Charlie. All Germans and all J . . . E . . . Ws."

The idea is familiar. Weiss insists on it in *The Investigation*, Hochhuth to a lesser extent in *The Deputy*. In similar circumstances men will behave in similar ways. The innocent will become the guilty, the victims the victimizers. It is all a question of opportunity, a matter of occasion. All men are at least partially guilty, at least potential aggressors, exploiters, killers.

Shaw wants to say this, of course, but also something more. It is how he combines the two that lends the play its early if distinctly flawed fascination. That and its not too subtly worn aura of intellectual mystery story. The game is called "Who is Arthur Goldman?"

Before continuing his deliberate confusion of the factors surrounding Goldman's real identity, Shaw drops a few more clues, has Goldman, for no apparent reason, cry out in anguish, then refer to "an old wound opening up." But, a moment later, he is neither screaming nor especially concerned with the "wound." "I got the image," he tells Charlie. "It's the details that bother me." It does not prevent him from getting on with the brochure, from being measured for "a blue gaberdine with a removable fur." In the meantime, another part of his mind is working out the "details" for the extraordinary events that are to come, events that, he now realizes, obviate any concern over whether the flower man *was* his cousin or not.

Goldman tells Charlie he will be making phone calls to the Vatican, Cairo, and Jerusalem. Then he sends him out of the room. When he is gone, he takes off his shirt and begins to sing softly:

> *what bells will ring for those who died*
> *like sheep?*

148

dies irae, dies illa
solvet saeclum in favilla,
what bells will ring for those who died
defiled?
for those who died in excrement?
rest eternal grant them
light eternal shine upon them.

After which he holds the end of a lighted cigar under his left armpit.

In the next scene, following a mysterious visit to Buenos Aires, he insists that from now on Charlie must address him as colonel. He also has another concern: "Dorff might just be eliminated." That would be too bad: he has done his research, laid out his case. But what research and what case? Within a few minutes the questions seemingly become academic. There are two men across the street in a Cadillac and they are watching the building. The phone rings and when Goldman hangs up, he tells the frightened Charlie to go downstairs to invite the two men up: "Tell 'em I have to find peace with my former enemies. . . . Tell 'em it's for the youth of Germany."

Is Goldman, then, Dorff, a German, a Nazi, not a Jew? So it seems, for the two young men who enter his apartment, guns drawn, followed by a woman holding a gun against Charlie's back, are obviously Israeli agents. One of them goes to check the secret room, which in the novel Goldman refers to as his "museum," where it is discovered he has a stool, a table, cartons of chocolate bars, and a copy of *Mein Kampf*.

Goldman makes an attempt to bribe Mrs. Rosen for his life—a million dollars; three. Seven million if she will wait a few days. But, she says, "not Christ's blood would buy it. Not from me." The two men remove a phial of poison from Goldman's mouth. They find the scar left by the burning cigar under his left arm; they check his collarbone and left kneecap against X-rays, his likeness against a photograph, even his cap size and his handwriting.

MRS. ROSEN: You are Adolf Karl Dorff. . . . If you cooperate you will be given a fair trial and the benefit

149

of legal counsel. . . . He was a Colonel in the Einsatz-
gruppen, the mobile killing unit of the S.S.

He protests that he is an American citizen, but it is to no avail.
He has no choice but to go with them.

But it is not to be quite that neat and clear-cut: not yet
another trial of yet another German war criminal protesting
that all that he did—if indeed he did anything—was done because of his orders, that he bore neither animus toward the Jews
nor any responsibility for their murder. For Goldman is not
Eichmann, not even an Eichmann-like figure. And he has no
aspiration to be.

Act 2 finds Goldman in an Israeli jail cell. There is one
question uppermost in Mrs. Rosen's mind: "Why did you pretend to be Jewish?" Goldman ignores it; he has his own points
to make. One of them—a very pivotal one—is the contention
that, unlike Eichmann, he was not a "clerk"; *he* is not going to
employ as a defense the insistence that everything was the result
of "orders" from higher up, that he was merely a cog in the
wheel that ground millions to death: "Issued my own orders,
plotted my own plots, had a ball. You follow?"

If Mrs. Rosen does, she gives no sign of it, returning time
after time to her question about why he pretended to be
Jewish. Again, however, Goldman insists on his own form and
forum; he is not merely the protagonist, but the author and
director of the drama in which he plays:

> I'm not here to plead I took orders. I had initiative.
> First honest man who's stood in your dock. Like you
> got the Fuehrer himself in here.

Still she keeps insisting, until finally he tells her he pretended
to be Jewish because he made the acquaintance of "old-Ameri-
can-Jewish-Uncle-Hymie's nephew," Arthur Goldman, in
Germany; he got to know him so well "I called him 'Cousin.'
Perhaps he was, Cousin."

But now he is tiring of all this. He announces to her that he
will waive his rights to protection as an American citizen and
face an authorized court. He will decline legal aid because he

150

wants to "present such a case as will interest the new generation." He has, however, one surprising condition: he must be
permitted to wear his freshly brushed Nazi uniform and jack-
boots. But something slips out—or does it?

> MRS. ROSEN: How did you manage to convince Hymie
> Goldman that you were his nephew, Arthur?
>
> GOLDMAN: Family likeness. . . .
>
> MRS. ROSEN: D'you mean you were related?
>
> GOLDMAN: Cousins. All cousins. My Aunt Judith and
> my Momma Sarah.

Is it only another of Goldman's, and Shaw's, red herrings,
only another effort to further blur the image of Goldman-
Dorff? It takes a bit longer to emerge. In the meantime, Goldman would rather talk of his first wife, Marlene, and of how the
Fuehrer—"Addy," as he says they called each other—appre-
ciated her. Regrettably, he admits, he lost touch with her.

In the courtroom itself, it momentarily appears the initiative
may be taken from Goldman. The prosecutor is determined to
try "the whole tragedy of Jewry"; it is to be his "central
concern." Just as he is about to make a "personal observation"
from his bulletproof glass booth, Goldman is disconcerted. There
is someone in the audience whom he recognizes: "Just seen Mrs.
Dorff out there. . . . And they told me she was dead." Eventually he gets back to the matter at hand:

> What are we interested in here, Your Honor, justice
> or the sufferings of the Jewish people? . . . If I under-
> stand justice, Your Honor, it's nobody's suffering
> that should be on trial here, it's what I done. . . . I,
> Your Honor, I am your central concern. . . . I mean,
> what's got to be proved, Your Honor—that I'm not fit
> to live.

They begin to call the witnesses. All testify to Goldman-
Dorff's guilt, to the deaths he was responsible for, to the family
members he shot before their eyes. Goldman acknowledges it

151

all—with pride and no little scorn for his victims, "sheep" who kept "gettin' on cattle trains and goin' to quarries and such like." What he doesn't understand, he tells the judge, "is why the Prosecutor does not demand the exposure of all the German authorities who permitted me to get on with my German work, and all those Jews who helped me?" He has a list of many of them—West German civil servants and businessmen, ministers and priests, doctors, lawyers, generals, and housewives. He begins to read it, but before he can get beyond the first name it is ruled "not admissible evidence." Some toes are not to be stepped on, some old coals not to be raked over.

Shaw obviously thinks they should be, that a guilt that may be—very likely is—distributable should be distributed; that the manufacturer of yesterday, often the manufacturer of today, the priest who looked the other way, or the politician who managed to emerge with his hands relatively—apparently—clean, also was culpable. Is it possible that all men are Nazis?

> So we're all Jews. All Germans. . . . In the camps, fellas . . . you all got to be members of the Party. . . . All of you. You follow? Very few exceptions. You'd gotten to believe in our German superiority, you tortured your own traitors. . . . You got to love us. You follow? And as for the Pope. Don't think he won't go back on all this dispensin'. Wait for the usual pall of silence, fellas.

One does not ask for "answers" to why it all happened—answers are perhaps impossible. What one does look for is some shaft of at least momentary illumination, some suggestion of new insight. It is here that Shaw fails. *The Man in the Glass Booth* is most of all "clever." In a serious kind of way. It takes a theme that has been used time and again in the past three decades and uses it yet once more, but without adding anything; at least without saying anything. Inevitably, one begins to resent its very cleverness, all those symbols and metaphors wandering about in search of an informing intelligence—or perhaps a sensibility—to transform them.

152

There is, however, a moment, a brilliant moment, late in the play, when Goldman-Dorff delivers a long monologue to the court. It is a paean to Hitler, to what he meant to the German people at a moment in history and why he was able to so completely capture their loyalty—why, Shaw suggests, another Hitler might capture ours today:

> People of the world, let me speak to you of my Fuehrer with love. . . . When he spoke . . . he would bang out his right arm like a hammer, louder and louder and louder he spoke, a torrent, a waterfall, the climax was shouted and shouted, out and up and beyond, and the end was absolute. Silence. Utter silence. A great wide sweep of the right arm and so to the tremendous cry, the vast overwhelming cry, the cry of love from the people. . . . Heil Hitler. . . . Do I see you begin to raise your hands? Do I hear you stamp your feet? . . . People of Israel . . . people of Israel, if he had chosen you . . . if he had chosen *you* . . . *you* also would have followed where he led.

And perhaps this is where the play has led. It is almost certainly where it should have ended. What follows—the picking up of pieces, the tying together of loose ends—says no more.

An old woman emerges from the audience to announce that "this man is not Dorff" and that she cannot let him continue. He is "enjoying himself too much." He, in fact, *is* Arthur Goldman and he is German-Jewish, a survivor of the camps. Dorff was perhaps his cousin; although cruelty personified, he did give him extra food, which Goldman distributed to his fellow prisoners. And, at the end of the war, when the Germans had fled, he, Dorff, came back and began methodically to shoot the prisoners in the nape of the neck and to throw their bodies into the snow. But the Russians, four young soldiers on large horses and wearing fur hats, arrived in time to save many of them. And one of them picked up Dorff and threw him onto the wire.

And we all ran out and tore at Dorff. We tore him to
pieces. But I remember thinking: Mr. Goldman has
stayed in the hut.

So it is all a "mistake." Goldman, with his millions, has
contrived it all: bribed Israeli agents; planted the X-rays, the
photographs, the handwriting samples; arranged for the forged
records; made the anonymous phone calls that led to his being
tracked down; burned the flesh under his arm so that they
would think the scar concealed an SS insignia.

But *why* did he do it? Did he merely wish a forum from
which to proclaim the collective guilt of mankind or of the
German nation? Did he simply wish to have on trial—finally to
have on trial—someone who would acknowledge responsibility
and provide a true picture of the mentality that prevailed in
those days, rather than an automaton only "taking orders?"
Was he involved in an act of atonement—and for what? Did he
view himself as some sort of Christ-surrogate?

All these, of course, and that is the play's major weakness.
Encompassing everything, it embodies nothing fully, becomes a
muddled rehashing of clichés, so diffuse in its effect that it
almost might be said not to have one. Goldman's own answer to
the *why* of his actions only serves to confound the question:

> Wanted to make some offering for them—something
> they'd understand. . . . I chose ya because I knew ya.
> I chose ya because you're smart. I chose ya because
> you're chosen. I chose ya for remembrance.

But who is this "I," this figure who goes on to tell of how he
in turn tortured and killed Germans after his release? Does he
see himself as God, a god, explaining, expiating? (In the novel,
he does in fact cry into the microphone, "I am Christ, the
chosen of God; offer me vinegar. I am the King of the Jews.")
When, finally, he locks himself in his glass booth, innocent by
their standards, is he even more guilty by his own? In the novel,
he insists, "This is not a rabbinical school. There is no 'why'
here." But today, in this context, *why* is the only question. To
deny and diffuse it, as Shaw has, into an intellectual party
game, meets neither historical nor theatrical imperatives.

154

Those who follow us will report incompletely, perhaps misrepresent. I put on record that Comrade Trotsky planned every step of the rebellion. He led the Petrograd Soviet to victory.

Trotsky in Exile

Not long after its world premiere in Düsseldorf, Peter Weiss's *Trotsky in Exile* was denounced in *Literaturnaya Gazeta*, the organ of the Soviet Writers' Union, for its alleged historical distortion, false documentation, and misrepresentation of the events of "the Great October Socialist Revolution." For anyone familiar with the virtual excision of Trotsky from Soviet history, the attack on Weiss by his fellow Marxists came as no surprise. As Weiss acknowledged in a subsequent "open letter," his account "does not correspond to the picture as it has been drawn in the Soviet Union for more than four decades." It is, however, he asserts, "not a falsification but an attempt at restoring just historical proportions."*

If anything is needed with Trotsky, whether in the theatre or the Soviet history books, it would seem to be "proportion." Viewed by many Western historians as the practical architect of the October Revolution and by others as its tragic hero, but by

---

*"An Open Letter to the *Literaturnaya Gazeta*" (Frankfurt am Main: Suhrkamp Verlag, 1971).

the rewriters of Soviet history as an opportunist and a traitor, he was nothing if not enigmatic: an activist who not only failed, but declined, to act at precisely the moment when it not only might have brought him to power, but also kept the Soviet Union more nearly on "the Leninist road." Eloquent, energetic, a passionate, at times arrogant, defender of his position throughout almost all of his life, a man in almost every way superior to his rival, Stalin, he lacked the one necessary thing the man from Soviet Georgia possessed: the lust for *personal* power. (Lenin, in his way, also lacked it, but the time and the circumstances were as vastly different as the men.)

It is not, however, this Lev Davidovich Bronstein (Trotsky) who emerges in *Trotsky in Exile*, but Trotsky the dialectician and theorist, Trotsky the prophet. It is, as Weiss told *The Times* of London (June 21, 1969), a play "about socialism for social- ists . . . a drama about revolutions." Regrettably, though it has its moments as dialectic, it is almost as heavy going theatrically as Weiss's own description suggests.

Trotsky in Exile spans some forty years, cutting back and forth in time from Trotsky's exile in the penal colony of Verkholensk (1901) to his assassination by an agent of the Soviet GPU (secret police) in Mexico in 1940. It is almost circular in structure and cinematic in conception, encompassing fifteen scenes, of which only a handful achieve genuine thea- trical life.

Trotsky is seated at his desk, reading a manuscript, pen in hand. It is a "room that could be anywhere," and in the course of the play it will be many places, the last of them—the image also of the first—the study of the fortress-like Mexican villa in which he lived during his final years of exile and in which the assassin struck.

But before that history and dialectic must be paid their due. Weiss begins in 1928, when Trotsky, already fallen from the role and stature he enjoyed while Lenin lived, is to be deported to Alma Ata (Turkestan). He will not, however, go without a final gesture. With the police on his doorstep, he announces:

> The Political Bureau is trying to make the banishment
> look like a voluntary agreement. That's what the

people have been told. Important to destroy this legend. To show the true facts. And in a way that can't be hushed up or misrepresented. We'll force the enemy to use violence.

But it is to no avail. Through the next dozen years, Trotsky will remain a hero, a legend, and a rallying point for many Soviet dissidents; a figure who is idolized, his every sentence devoured, by many outside the Soviet Union. But the moment when he, in conjunction with Lenin, altered the shape of not only Russian, but world, history is past. The heir apparent to Soviet leadership has become an outcast, one of the few, perhaps the only, truly tragic figure to be spawned by the many tragic events of the time.

With the second of his fifteen scenes, Weiss reverts to more or less chronological order, following Trotsky from his 1901 Siberian exile, with its endless debates on revolutionary theory, through his escape and first meeting with Lenin, in London in 1902. By now, Lev Bronstein has adopted the name of Trotsky, the name of his prison warder in Odessa, the name by which history will know him. He and Lenin debate "the question being asked all over Russia: what should the party do? Is it to think, decide, and act for the proletariat?" Whether, as Lenin contends, a "bourgeois revolution is the necessary first step," or, as Trotsky, the twenty-three-year-old enthusiast, insists, "the proletariat is ready to go."

They were to disagree many times in the next fifteen years, the years before the revolution: at the Brussels conference of 1903, over whether "strict centralism" of what was then the Russian Social Democratic Labor party was necessary; over definitions of "democracy" and membership in the party. At the end, the party is split between the Bolsheviks and the Mensheviks. In the years after Lenin's death in 1924, as Stalin constructs Trotsky's political coffin, the fact that he sided with the Mensheviks will cost him dearly.

Succeeding scenes show Trotsky addressing the crowd during the cruelly repressed rising of January, 1905, after which he again finds himself in Siberia, this time sentenced for life. Again, Weiss concerns himself more with dialectic than with drama, with talk of action that has already occurred rather than with the action itself. Although the Social Democrats of the time are known to have spent countless hours in heated theoretical and tactical arguments, it is difficult if not impossible to re-create their heat and fervor on a stage nearly seventy years later. Only at rare moments does the play really come alive, really dramatize the conflict among all these fiercely committed revolutionaries—not only Lenin and Trotsky, but Plekhanov, Martov, Kamenev, Sverdlov, Zinoviev, Bukharin, and the many others Weiss brings on to offer their theories on the politics and ethics of Russian social democracy.

Trotsky was to remain in exile for nearly ten years on this occasion; to discuss with Lenin in Zurich in 1914 their continued conflicting opinions on the best basis on which to approach revolution, with Trotsky insisting he "wanted to bring the groups together" and Lenin that "there's no room for compromise." On one thing they can agree: the "imperialistic war" must be turned into a socialist revolution; its soldiers must point their weapons "not against the wage slaves of other countries, but against [their] own governments."

Only with the October Revolution itself does the play take on additional drama and dimension. Workers, sailors, and soldiers mill about waiting for their catalyst, Trotsky, to rally them to a revolution in which everything is "so terribly quiet," a revolution the "bourgeoisie" prefer not as yet to see. But it is there. Those "who always stood at the back, miles behind, invisible," are "now at the front," and with their emergence, the bourgeoisie will "start to tremble."

At the Smolny Institute on the Nevsky Prospekt, there is chaos but also history in the making. Lenin, having insisted that the moment was at hand for an armed rising, sees the long-planned-for triumph on the brink of being. It is not a time to hesitate. To wait "would be a betrayal of the revolution."

> Opportunities for armed rising must be seized as they come. You can't keep them for later. History gives no pardon to revolutionaries who put off till tomorrow what they can win today.

Telephones ring; soldiers and sailors come dashing in with

158

reports and receive orders. The state bank and the telephone exchange have been occupied; the electricity and water works and the main post office have been secured. Trotsky, the tactician, the activist, now firmly on Lenin's side, gives orders, sends messages, calls out troops. It has all happened almost too rapidly. Even for Lenin. "So soon after persecution, exile—power. It makes one giddy." (What Lenin in fact said was much the same: "The transition from the state of illegality, being driven in every direction, to power—is too rough. It makes one dizzy." He then reportedly "made the sign of the cross before his face."*)

But the "giddiness" is not for long. Lenin knows a government must be formed. As its chairman he proposes Trotsky. When Sverdlov insists Trotsky was "too long outside the party" to assume so lofty a post, Lenin argues:

> There are no better Bolsheviks than Trotsky. He stands at the head of the Petrograd Soviet. I state this categorically. There are no official records of these days. Only scribbled notes and verbal orders. None of us has time to write history. Who knows how many of us will still be here in the next weeks, months? Those who follow us will report incompletely, perhaps misrepresent. I put on record that Comrade Trotsky planned every step of the rebellion. He led the Petrograd Soviet to victory.

But Trotsky declines, accepting instead the commissariat for foreign affairs. For the immediate future, and despite ideological disputes, Lenin and he will be, as Louis Fischer described it, the "senior and junior partners in the management of the revolution."†

Weiss has the two men engage in a long colloquy on the next day. It reflects more hindsight than the hectic and improvised character of those days. Lenin wonders whether the October

*Leon Trotsky, *Lenin* (New York, 1925), p. 102.
†Louis Fischer, *The Life of Lenin* (New York: Harper and Row, 1964), p. 181.

Revolution could have taken place without them. Trotsky is uncertain. When Lenin asks him whether the quarrel between the two of them is "over now," Trotsky denies it was a quarrel; rather, it was a "mutual testing of strength" in which they "pushed each other forward. Took over each other's ideas. Ironed out differences of opinion. . . . In the future too there'll be controversy, contradictions. Would we be Marxists otherwise?"

But Lenin is concerned about other aspects of that future. "I've got only a few more years," he says. (His first stroke occurred some four and a half years later.)

> The others, they won't put up with you when I'm no longer here. Your self-assurance, your international interests. They'll call it arrogance, vanity. They'll band together and throw you out. Then we'll see what the revolutionary masses are worth. Whether they'll come out on your side.

Using cinematic license, Weiss cuts to the future as the act ends. Soldiers appear to take Trotsky away. He is charged with "having taken part in counter-revolutionary activity through the organization of an illegal anti-Soviet party." It is January, 1929, and Trotsky is to be "deported from the territories of the Soviet Republic."

The opening scene of the second act finds him again in exile, again engaging in one of the endless debates that filled the hours for the Soviet emigré. Blumkin, one of his supporters, tells him

> the name of Trotsky is being scratched from the records of the revolution. . . . Coming generations will know nothing about you. History is being rewritten. All that remains is He [Stalin]. From the beginning it was *he* alone who stood at Lenin's side.

Although it betrays an excessive prescience, the statement itself is of course true. Countless photographs and paintings, not to mention history books and encyclopedias, were to be altered or created to remove Trotsky or to show Stalin in a major role, a

160

role he in no wise played during the October Revolution, when he was a distinctly secondary figure. Some of this repainting and airbrushing of history remains very much in evidence in the Soviet museums of today.

Employing his fluid framework, Weiss again reverts to the past, to the death of Lenin. But before that, there is yet another ideological discussion between the two men, this time over the dangers of bureaucracy within the party. The now seriously ill Lenin wants Trotsky to lead the fight against it. And, he says, "Stalin must be got out. Much too much power in his hands. He's just waiting for me to go. To grab the party for himself alone." He tells Trotsky that it is he who is the "most capable," and that he must fight:

> Why don't you speak? Why, when I'm about to go, do you suddenly become so weak and helpless? Why do you pull back? . . . Do you think they'll run after you? Proclaim you my successor? . . . You must be firm, unyielding. They'll see you're right in the end. Our revolution must spread out into world revolution, or it will die.

Like virtually all of the meticulously researched material in the play, this reflection of Lenin's attitude at the time of his death is historically accurate, though the statement concerning Stalin and his qualified praise of Trotsky in fact occurred in his so-called Testament, a letter to the forthcoming party congress in which he called for, among other things, the removal of Stalin from his post of party general secretary. After Lenin's death, the Testament was for years suppressed in the Soviet Union, not finally to be published there until 1956, following Khrushchev's celebrated "secret speech" denouncing Stalin at the Twentieth Party Congress.

That they did not "run after" Trotsky, but rather kept him on the run is a matter of history. Equally so is the fact that for practical purposes Trotsky's own role was now as "played out" as that of the Mensheviks and others he had scornfully consigned to the "dustbins of history" in those heady days of

October, 1917. Though he would remain in the Soviet Union until 1929, his underestimation of Stalin was to prove fatal.

From that time on, he would write, speak, and attract disciples, but with Lenin's death he became a prophet not a mover of history, moving from one place of exile to another—to Turkey, to France, to Norway, and finally to Mexico. Much of the remainder of the play centers on an exposition of his doctrine of world revolution. In 1935, in Grenoble, he is visited by a group of students from Paris. Since Weiss numbers among them French, German, Indochinese, South American, and Afro-American, there is ample occasion for "the prophet outcast," as Isaac Deutscher called him, to expound and to be challenged by the young. As dialectic, it has its occasional moments, as drama almost none.

Scene 13, "Enemy of the People," finds Trotsky and his wife, Natalia, in Norway. In the background the 1936 Moscow trials, during which Trotsky was condemned in absentia, are going on. The procession of witnesses—Kamenev, Zinoviev, Radek, and others—testify to Trotsky's "traitorous activities" and efforts "to undermine our economic and military strength, to encourage an armed attack by the fascists, to help foreign aggressors seize and share out our territory. . . ." And so the prosecutor drones on. Trotsky insists to Natalia that "every point can be refuted." But the documents are in Paris; he is in Hönnefoss—at least he is for the moment. He is soon to be expelled and to settle in Mexico.

It remains only to play out the last scenes, the final days in a life that may have been tragic, but also was marked by opportunities ignored, moments not seized, and failures of nerve. (Though, for instance, he later was to accuse Stalin of poisoning Lenin, Trotsky himself participated in the suppression of the Testament, something he apparently could justify to himself on the grounds that the party was always right—ultimately.)

In the penultimate scene, the police have just arrived to investigate an unsuccessful attempt on Trotsky's life. He lives in a virtual fortress, surrounded by bodyguards, in which any stranger is automatically suspect. Frank Jacson was one such stranger, but by this time has worked his way into the at least partial confidence of Trotsky and his wife. ("Jacson" was a

162

pseudonym, apparently for one Ramon Mercader, the son of a Spanish Communist who had close connections with the GPU, whose agent he became in the plot to assassinate Trotsky.*)

"Just by being alive I disturb the present leaders," Trotsky tells the Mexican painter Diego Rivera, who with André Breton has come to visit him. After an extended discussion of why the defendants at the Moscow trials behaved as they did, he contends that:

> What has happened shows, not that socialism is wrong, but that our revolutionary acts have exposed our weakness and inexperience. We have not succeeded in overcoming human frailty, human cowardice, human baseness. Remember, the experiment in the Soviet Union is hardly more than twenty years old. . . . Against socialism that other system still stands firm: the system of absolute baseness, absolute greed, absolute selfishness. That system cannot change. . . . But socialism, in spite of the crimes committed in its name, can change. . . . If death were to strike me today, I could say I had worked for the exploited and colonized masses in the permanent struggle for liberation.

If death were to strike me today . . . Trotsky has said. And a moment later, Jacson appears with an essay he has written and says he wants Trotsky to read. He wears a hat and, despite the heat, holds a raincoat pressed against his side. When Natalia leaves them alone, Trotsky sits down at the desk and bends over the manuscript. It is the position he was in at the beginning of the play. Moments later, Jacson stands behind him, an ice axe poised to strike his head. The lights go down.

Even as a play "about socialism for socialists," the effectiveness of *Trotsky in Exile* is questionable. Weiss's Trotsky, prophet and fount of all revolutionary wisdom, possesses a degree of foresight and infallibility that permits no effective challenge. Whether talking to Mensheviks or Bolsheviks, Dada-

*Issac Deutscher, *The Prophet Outcast: Trotsky: 1929-1940* (New York: Oxford University Press, 1963).

163

ists or students, old friends or old enemies; whether proclaiming the need for permanent world revolution or exhorting a crowd toward its role in the dictatorship of the proletariat, Trotsky is never other than right (even Lenin was known to have made mistakes on occasion!). Although such ideological argumentation can be, and on occasion is, interesting, indeed fascinating, it requires genuine contention, the possibility of defeat for *either* side, to make it dramatically convincing and effective.

It is reported that when the play had its Düsseldorf world premiere in 1970, a group of angry students interrupted the performance, causing Weiss to cancel the second act. The students announced to the audience that they would reenact what had taken place thus far. With that, one of them, identified as Trotsky, set himself up as a bowler and the others crowded together. "Trotsky" toppled them en masse with the first roll. A bit lacking in subtlety, perhaps, but as an image for the play's ideological "debate" there's a lot to be said for it.

In the end, *Trotsky in Exile*'s almost total reliance on argumentation and analysis rather than action and characterization is fatal. Even Trotsky, with most of the qualities of the tragic hero, a man of many and intriguing parts, never becomes more than a spokesman for his ideas, a visionary whose anticipation of the events to come is awe-inspiring. That he to some extent was is not in question. That he was the one-dimensional figure, the cerebral creation Weiss makes him, is. Accurate history—and the play is almost entirely accurate historically—and ideological conviction are simply not enough, not when they are embodied in puppets. There is a moment early in the second act when Trotsky's daughter Zinaida, after a long recapitulation of what is then taking place in the Soviet Union, suddenly wonders whether all the deaths and imprisonments, even those in their own family, have ever reached him, caused him, caused this "stuffed dummy," distress. It is symbolic of the play's weakness that we never know the answer.

*It seems to me that I have
been half expecting this man
since I came.*

Murderous Angels

Although Conor Cruise O'Brien calls *Murderous Angels* "a political tragedy and comedy in black and white," it would be more accurate—if less enticing—to term it a political morality play. Pitting the forces of Peace against the forces of Freedom, O'Brien asks the audience to see his characters as figures on a chess board, governed, and sometimes manipulated, by forces external to them, pawns in the ongoing struggle between black and white, rich and poor, expediency and an ideal. But they are also men, and that is the beginning of the problem.

"The angels are the great and noble abstractions represented by the protagonists: Peace in the case of Hammarskjöld, Freedom in the case of Lumumba," O'Brien says in a preface to the published version. They "are not to be thought of as the 'real' characters of that name but as personages shaped by the imitation of a real action associated with their names." It is a problematic tactic and for many reasons, some historical, some theatrical, it falls considerably short of working.

O'Brien was for a time head of the Irish delegation to the UN. *Murderous Angels* covers some of the same ground that was explored in *To Katanga and Back*, which grew out of his 1961 mission to secessionist Katanga as Hammarskjöld's representative. O'Brien knew many of the actual figures he depicts and had occasion to observe the actions of the theoretically symbolic or representative types he invents.

165

"The germ of *Murderous Angels*," he writes, "is the conception that Hammarskjöld, for exalted and convincing reasons, and in the service of humanity deliberately brings about the downfall and refrains from preventing the death of Patrice Lumumba, which in its turn precipitates his own downfall and death." O'Brien views Hammarskjöld as "a gifted, sincere and even exalted idealist who was prepared, if necessary, to act ruthlessly and unscrupulously in pursuit of his ideal, and who found, in the Congo, adequate reasons for believing it necessary to act in this way." Unfortunately, one of the weaknesses of the play is that instead of *this* central figure, its Hammarskjöld is seldom other than a puppet mouthing lofty sentiments that recall *Markings* and other writings, and philosophizing on the endless play of ends and means. "I never heard Hammarskjöld talk in this way," O'Brien admits, "but it is quite clear that this was his habit of thought, and the presentation of this was essential to the 'imitation of the action' which I undertook."

O'Brien's Lumumba, on the other hand, is a moderately believable if exaggerated character, perhaps because O'Brien's sympathies so clearly lie more with the "angel" Freedom than with its adversary Peace. Both angels are equally murderous.

Many of the characters in *Murderous Angels* are intended as embodiments of a class or an attitude: Baron d'Auge, who according to O'Brien, "began to take shape as a figure who would express, with lucidity and a certain candor, the motivations and political and other calculations of a financier defending his claim to the resources of the Congo in the circumstances of 1960-1961"; Monsignor Polycarpe, "intended to typify the Europeans of Katanga collectively—including the clergy—in their relation to the powers that then were"; James Bonham, who "comes from the area of 'area studies' . . . [where] a scholar can convert his knowledge of a people or a region into utility to a state or a company . . . and some take a romantic pleasure in wearing the voluminous cloak and diminutive dagger of the academic mercenary."

It is July, 1960, soon after the establishment of the Congo as an independent republic. Congolese soldiers have mutinied and Belgian paratroops have intervened to restore order in the mineral-rich province of Katanga. In the play, they have inter-

166

vened at the request of the fictional Baron d'Auge, president of the Société Universelle, an international consortium with "a number of financial, industrial and commercial enterprises, which are not without importance." D'Auge's interest is obvious: Katanga contains copper, uranium, and cobalt, among other commodities. On the day following the Belgian landing in Elisabethville, Moïse Tshombe has proclaimed the independence of Katanga.

But in Leopoldville, Lumumba remains prime minister. Unlike the situation in Katanga—"white power with a black front"—his brand of independence means genuine black power. Obviously, it holds more attraction for the vast majority of the Congolese. But to achieve it, and to retain his power and appeal, Lumumba must recapture the initiative and regain control of the defecting province. To do so, he needs outside aid, which he requests from the United Nations, to "protect the territory of the Congo against the present external aggression." How will Hammarskjöld respond? By sending UN troops to expel the Belgians or by siding with "white power," European financial, and American political interests, to bring about the prickly Lumumba's downfall? D'Auge sets the scene:

> The Congo is vast and amorphous: the United Nations represents the nebulous about to plunge into the amorphous. The resolutions are ambiguous: the Secretary-General is subtle, oblique and priest-like; Lumumba is violent, unstable and contagious; the international conjecture dark, complex and inscrutable. What is clear, however, is the existence of certain concrete interests, which my friends and I must seek to defend by all appropriate means available to us in these bizarre circumstances.

And so, d'Auge goes to Katanga, where in August, 1960, he meets with Monsignor Polycarpe at his residence near Elisabethville. The priest is a power in the territory, if not a power to d'Auge. He can help in lining up the kind of welcome the consortium deems it advisable for Hammarskjöld to receive when he flies in to see Tshombe. Polycarpe has his curiosity about the secretary general. "Is it true that he is a pederast?" he inquires, one of several references in the play to Hammarskjöld's alleged homosexuality. But d'Auge has other things on his mind, and he elects to explain Hammarskjöld in other terms:

> It appears from [his diary] that he is in the habit of thinking of himself as a kind of Messiah. . . . A saint, a king, a hero. . . . Crucifixion seems to come into it. . . . The man has what they call a "built-in compulsion" to *save* things. . . . What he has to save at present is the Congo. . . . And it is in the power of the Americans—and not at all in the power of anyone else except them—to create and maintain the conditions in which he can go on believing he is saving the Congo. . . . His relation to America is rather like that of man to God; he has free will, but only under and within the omnipotence of the higher power, and it is in these conditions that he must work out his salvation.

Faithful to their masters' bidding, Tshombe and Godefroid Munongo, his minister of the interior, meet Hammarskjöld at the Elisabethville airport. The event is complete with dancing, tribal chiefs in full regalia, drumming, and African soldiers in dress uniform—all designed to impress on Hammarskjöld "the inscrutably indigenous character of our local institutions." And there is something else: an enormous green, white, and red flag with copper crosslets, the banner of Katanga. Hammarskjöld and Tshombe are photographed beneath it.

The implied recognition, albeit unintentional, of the breakaway province infuriates Lumumba and he requests aid from what he views as the only possible source, the Soviet Union. Hammarskjöld is not unaware of Lumumba's probable reaction. However, his self-imposed messianic role now emerging ever more strongly, he tells Diallo Diop, his black Senegalese assistant (a wholly fictitious character, according to O'Brien) with whom it is suggested he may have other than professional relations: "The hope of the black men may be drawn for a time to fight against the hope of all mankind. . . .

The United Nations is the hope of all mankind." The Congo cannot be permitted to turn into another Korea and perhaps the spark to a third world war. To prevent that, he will accept contamination, compromise, and betrayal of and by himself.

Lumumba is outraged. Although Hammarskjöld's staff makes repeated efforts to contact him by phone and to set up a meeting, he adamantly refuses. Finally, the secretary general himself comes on the phone. Lumumba's secretary and mistress (apparently entirely fictional mistress), Madame Rose, attempts to get him to take the call:

> He says it's literally a matter of life and death . . .
> And he asked me to be sure to repeat those seven
> words: "Literally a matter of life and death."

> LUMUMBA: Very well, tell him to drop dead.

From that moment, if not before, Lumumba's death is simply a matter of time. Hammarskjöld meets with the American ambassador in Leopoldville and is told: "As far as Russians in the Congo are concerned, Washington makes it clear that they will not permit that. Whatever is necessary to stop it—they say—must be done. Whatever is necessary." Since the Russians have been invited in by the legitimate head of the Congolese government, what is necessary is his removal and replacement by someone who will invite the Russians to leave. If not that, the ambassador suggests, there may indeed be another Korea and the UN will be discredited and impotent.

The Americans have made arrangements for Lumumba's fall; specifically, that he will be dismissed by President Kasavubu, "whom our Treasury has supplied with arguments that he found convincing," and that a new prime minister will be appointed.

"The context you make for me is such that if I am to serve the United Nations, and the peace, I must help you to destroy Patrice Lumumba," Hammarskjöld responds. And by "destroy," it is made clear, the American means precisely that: "He will remain a danger for us as long as he lives. . . . We cannot allow him to leave the Congo and stir up trouble for us elsewhere in Africa. . . . Having thrown Patrice Lumumba to his enemies [by failing to protect him effectively, we] will then stand aside while those enemies, chosen by us, put him to death." Hammarskjöld agrees. It is not, he says, his business to remain unscathed or to keep his hands clean; it is his responsibility to defend "the hopes that humanity has placed in the United Nations."

When, two and one-half months later, Lumumba requests a plane—or a seat on a plane—to Stanleyville, even under guard, from the UN's chief representative in the Congo in order that he may be present at the burial of his daughter, he is refused. All else aside, Stanleyville is a hotbed of Lumumba supporters. He goes on his own and is captured. Hammarskjöld is asked by his aide in Leopoldville to authorize a UN detachment that has sufficient strength to free Lumumba from his captors, but refuses to do so. Lumumba is killed by the Katangese and his body disposed of in hydrochloric acid.

There is, O'Brien acknowledges in an appendix, no specific documentation concerning this request and its denial. It is but one of many such hypothetical positings on pivotal issues and, like some of the others, throws the play's credibility open to serious question. It is, however, likely that on at least two other occasions—at the Leopoldville and Elisabethville airports—UN forces stood by while Lumumba was maltreated by his captors.

When the news of Lumumba's death reaches the UN nearly a month later, there is a predictable furore on the part of many African states and that of the Soviet Union (which, in fact, described the event as "the culmination of Hammarskjöld's criminal activities," asserting that "the blood of Patrice Lumumba is on the hands of this henchman of the colonialists and cannot be removed"). Before the Security Council, Hammarskjöld insists there was no possibility for the UN to avoid Lumumba's death. "It was not in control of the situation." While Adlai Stevenson is addressing the Council, a riot breaks out among the spectators.

When Hammarskjöld returns to his office, where he finds Diop and the ubiquitous Bonham, he is the soul of cynicism— for the good of the cause. Where, before, it was one side that had to be indulged, now it is the other. "You see," he tells Bonham, "then, I was deaf in my left ear, my black ear; now I must be deaf in my right ear for a while. The white one." And

170

he does not regret it: "My honor is intact and unsullied because I did what I had to do for the high purpose to which I have dedicated my life, and for that high purpose only."

Even when he is confronted by one of the demonstrators, Lumumba's "junior wife," Madame Rose, and she spits in his face, he remains coolly above a display of emotion. She is, he says, "just another casualty of peace preservation."

All that remains is for Hammarskjöld himself to die. With a new American administration in power (and the faith of the Third World to be reclaimed), a UN resolution calling for the "use of force if necessary" to reunify the Congo, and the European consortium bent on maintaining its position, UN forces occupy public buildings in Katanga and declare the secession at an end.

Baron d'Auge confides to his colleagues that there are "cold feet in Washington":

> And when Washington gets cold feet, the United Nations loses a few toes. I think Hammarskjöld must be very nearly at the point where he will see that the service of his great ideal requires, once more, the dumping of some of his pals. Just one more turn of the screw, and I think we'll see Moïse restored to the throne of his ancestors.

And so one of them sees Hammarskjöld and convinces him he must fly to the Congo to see Tshombe. They agree on a meeting in Ndola and when Tshombe tells Munongo of it, the latter decides the moment is ripe to hijack the plane and kidnap Hammarskjöld. Kidnap or . . .? Colonel Zbyre, a hired mercenary, laughs: "But are many chances for something interesting to happen." As they are boarding the plane, Hammarskjöld tells Bonham: "You and I are both part of a pattern of which this journey . . . draws the threads together." With that, he takes off, only to die in a mysterious explosion in the sky over Ndola, bringing to a conclusion an equation he has cited earlier: "Who says 'A' says 'B.' We both said A, in our own quite different accents, and now here is B. Which we have to say also. Leaving C to be said by someone else."

171

O'Brien's evidence in both instances—the assassination of Lumumba and the death of Hammarskjöld—is largely circumstantial, some aspects of it more convincing than others. Exercising perhaps more than justifiable dramatic license, he at times makes the actions of the central figures more black and white than they likely were. There is also another difficulty, and it is not circumvented by his assertion that the principal figures of *Murderous Angels* "are not to be thought of as the 'real' characters of that name."

At what point does history end and fiction begin? The question arises more strongly here than in many other plays in the theatre of fact or even the theatre of controversy overall, for the simple reason that O'Brien's hypotheses are more suspect than those of, say, Kipphardt in *In the Matter of J. Robert Oppenheimer* or Stanley Greenberg in *Pueblo*. Is it enough simply to claim that Hammerskjöld and Lumumba and the remaining characters are symbolic or metaphorical, and then to arrange fact and fiction into some form of seamless garment?

O'Brien never really transforms his material from polemic to play, from argumentation to art. There is too much reliance on the Aristotelian license he cites: "Tragedy is an imitation, not of man but of an action and of a life. . . . Tragedians still keep to real names, the reason being that what is possible is credible." What is possible *is* credible and perhaps that suggests the question confronting *Murderous Angels* and similar plays. In dealing with historical figures, is what is possible and credible in the service of art also justifiable in the service of point-scoring? The line is admittedly a fine one.

Obviously, there is a question not simply of historical but of dramatic credibility. Of the characters, Lumumba alone possesses any appreciable *theatrical* life. He is flamboyant, proud, committed, and aggressively heterosexual. Hammarskjöld, on the other hand, is seldom more than a puppet mouthing his self-condemning brief, a position paper for the murderous white angel Peace when it comes in conflict with the black angel of Freedom. Playing God, prissily pedantic, cynical, sanctimonious, by implication homosexual, he is a complex character permitted no *human* depth or dimension.

Then, too, there are the innumerable areas of doubt—at times

172

of contradiction—that O'Brien's own appendix acknowledges. There is something at least faintly disingenuous about the elaborate rationale O'Brien has created, something of a desire to have it both ways: the freedom of fiction and the mantle of history. What is admitted in the "documentation" is denied in the play. *It* is all just too cut-and-dried, too black-and-white—a triumph of politics (read, American foreign policy and European financial interests) over people and the popular will. The effect is to reduce nearly all to the level of one-dimensional archetype or crude caricature, a situation that in the end deprives the events of credibility and results in both bad theatre *and* bad politics. This regardless of the significance of the broader questions the play raises.

One is left to wonder how much more convincing it would have been if O'Brien had borne in mind what he has the title character say in his *King Herod Explains*: "There is no politics at three o'clock in the morning." To be fully convincing, any play—at least any play of serious purpose—requires at least one three o'clock in the morning, one moment at which the realization of the consequences of our actions in human terms is acknowledged, if not necessarily acted upon. *Murderous Angels* has no such moment.

The fire's today.

The Plebeians Rehearse the Uprising

Although Günter Grass subtitles *The Plebeians Rehearse the Uprising* "A German Tragedy," he might as easily have called it "A Day in the Life of Bertolt Brecht." At least that's the aspect of the play that has attracted the greatest attention. The day— "the fateful date," as Grass puts it—is June 17, 1953, when the workers of East Berlin rose against the government of Walter Ulbricht. The fact that *The Plebeians* itself is pure fiction—and offered as such—does not alter the fact that Brecht's actions on that day, in that period, became a center of controversy and indignation. Although they weren't what Grass, deliberately disclaiming historical authenticity, makes them, it seems fair to speculate that at least some of the undercurrents, and perhaps much of the internal conflict he depicts, did exist. It seems even more fair to take a look at the play's actual theme: the tragic flaw in the German people that dooms its revolutions to failure.

On June 17, the construction workers on Stalin-Allee take to the streets in protest against the East German government's imposition of an increase of at least ten percent in the production norms. As this is going on, Brecht—the "Boss," as he is called in the play—and his Berliner Ensemble are rehearsing the first scene of *Coriolan*, the uprising of the plebeians (he was, in fact, rehearsing Strittmatter's *Katzgraben*, but, as Grass asserts, this was the period during which he was preparing his Shakespearean adaptation).

"The Boss's idea is to upgrade the plebeians and tribunes,

175

give Coriolanus class-conscious enemies," Litthenner, one of his assistants, says as they await the Boss's arrival to begin the rehearsal. "I know his thesis," replies Podulla, a second assistant. "No muddleheaded insurrectionists—conscious revolutionaries." The Boss arrives, but his actors and plebeians are more leisurely about the time. With typical Brechtian irony—and a foretaste of the Brechtian attitude—he remarks:

> Here we're rehearsing the revolution and the plebeians are late! Symbolism? No, plain sloppiness.

When they do arrive, it is with the news, "There's something cooking in town." But the Boss doesn't want to be interrupted. Besides, he insists, it's just "the usual parade." And, if today *is* something different, they will use that something different: tape it and observe "the beautiful seriousness of the plebeians" and learn something that they can use in their crowd scenes. As for their revolution: "No plan, no logic. You can't make a revolution with feeling."

Volumnia (patterned on Helene Weigel) appears. She, too, has come from the streets with a report of the uprising. Still, Brecht will have none of it. His theatre will stay open; at most there will be some broken windows. That's the worst that can happen with such "unrehearsed incompetence."

Eventually, three masons appear. They want Brecht to help them to draw up a manifesto. He is internationally known, "a name to reckon with," and "the boys up top" will listen to his words if not to theirs. They know only the trades they've learned; he can give their statement eloquence.

Brecht has nothing but scorn for them. Although Volumnia tells him, "A few words from you will give their stammering meaning," he instead goes about trying to draw the workers out on what has taken place so that he can use it in his production. They become disgruntled over his delay in helping them: "The fire's today." But Brecht does not believe anything will come of their rebellion: "You're going to march straight back where you came from."

Volumnia tries to persuade him that he is out of contact with the people, that the workers' mentality has changed. He is unconvinced. They have no plan, they have no leader. They haven't even occupied the radio station. His attitude is that of Coriolanus to the plebeians. He arrogantly disdains and cynically mocks them. Brecht, the Marxist revolutionary, the glory of the East German Communist state, has no time for amateur revolutionaries. He is as unlikely to bow to their demands as Shakespeare's proud aristocrat Coriolanus was to bow to the Roman plebeians. He is staging *Coriolan* in order to "instruct the public [in] how you make a revolution and how you don't," but, for the moment, the public is ignorant.

These revolutionaries are nothing but a collection of disorganized amateurs, and Brecht is loftily above them, an aesthete whose involvement with art has separated him from the realities of the moment, from the very proletariat he has for so long extolled. He thinks the workers should "go home and give your wives a hand." With their traditional German passion for order, they will, he scornfully says, even obey the keep-off-the-grass signs as they attempt to make a revolution. They will fail because they do not know how to use their power.

But Brecht is something more than this, as both subsequent scenes and reality make clear. He is involved in a double dilemma. Not only has his own genius set him apart from the people, but he is caught also in the trap of his relationship with a totalitarian state, an artist and an intellectual asked to become an activist. It is Grass's contention that this is his—and many others'—sin: they will theorize but refuse to get their hands dirty. (Grass himself has taken the other course, frequently campaigning and writing speeches for the Social Democratic party, only to be denounced by his fellow artists and intellectuals for writing short-term propaganda rather than long-term literature.)

However, as Erwin, the dramatic adviser, says, "great bastions are seldom taken at the first try." The revolutionaries continue to work on Brecht and he continues to see in them material for his art, for the scene of the rising of the plebeians, even when Volumnia tells him:

From this day on, which cries out for socialism
As do we all, you, I and he—

177

Every mechanic, mason, carpenter
Will call you traitor if you don't bestir yourself.

All he will say is, "What can I do? I can't stand revolutionaries who are afraid to walk on the grass." In the meantime, by
using them, by showing in *Coriolan* what shouldn't be done,
"we make it clear what the revolution demands." He will, he
tells the foreman, show them what they are doing out there. It
is not what they want. All they want is his name. "That'll make
everybody sit up and take notice."

The workers are not the only ones who want Brecht's help.
Kozanka, "the people's bard," as Volumnia sarcastically labels
him, arrives to enlist him on the side of the government: "To
you they'll listen. All I got was catcalls." It is, he reminds
Brecht, the state—the Democratic Republic, not the West—that
supports his theatre. "We're very grateful to our noble patron,"
Brecht says ironically. But he does nothing—at least not for the
moment.

Eventually, two others come from the strike committee. The
workers have grown tired of waiting for "the friend of the
downtrodden workers," as one of them sarcastically calls him.
They want him to write a strike call or an open letter, "a very
open letter." And, surprisingly, Brecht agrees. He dictates a
letter to Ulbricht, but it is not the letter they have sought so
eagerly:

No bloodshed. Kindly tell your soldiers that
Our citizens are only trying to see
Whether in an emergency our streets
Are wide enough to hold a revolution.
Then like good children they'll go home to mother
And eat potato pancakes for their supper.
But this much, comrade, should be evident,
Our streets and squares are more than adequate
For a rebellion that will end your state.

The letter is full of Brechtian irony, but as one of the
workers says, you could take it "in one way . . . or you could
take it in another way." And that is not good enough for them;

178

they decide to string them up—the Boss and Erwin—from their own spotbar. They get as far as putting the nooses around their necks but are talked out of it by a fable rendered by Erwin about the body's members rebelling against the belly (the state).

Just as Brecht and Erwin are about to leave, Brecht is confronted with something that changes his mind. A worker has hauled the Soviet flag from the Brandenburg Gate. Wounded and still carrying the flag, he is brought into the theatre. He tells his story and Brecht is transfixed. There is something else as well—a young hairdresser, passionately committed and unafraid. She calls them cowards, cowards who can't think of anything to do now that the Soviet tanks have begun to rumble in the streets and the government has begun to react with fire hoses and loudspeakers. But she, *she* could "cripple one of those things with a hairpin." Erwin tells Brecht, "She could have been written by you, Boss." "I'm afraid she was," he says:

> This little soprano trumpet wakens dreams
> That should be better left to sleep.

And well she might have been written by Brecht. When she was seventeen, she went to the theatre:

> That's where I sat when Katrin, mute
> Katrin, sat drumming on the roof.
> As now I scream. The tanks are coming!
> Come on, Boss. Come, and crawl out of that shell:
> And we'll put on a play for the whole world,
> Enacted in the street, on barricades.
> Molotov cocktails. Plaster in exhaust pipes.
> Their sight slits plugged until they zigzag
> Blindly and clash. They'll all be turned to scrap
> If you and I, the two of us,
> Just give Berlin the sign. Come on!

"We'll take the radio station and you'll speak!" she exhorts him. And, almost miraculously, he agrees. It is, however, too late; he has withheld his support for too long. Volumnia tells him that martial law has been declared and they had best look

179

to answers for some of the questions they are going to be asked. That quickly, the moment passes. "That was a short engagement," the hairdresser tells Brecht, and a moment later he is left alone on the stage, left alone to wonder. "This rubbish blocked/ My way, I stumbled and I went no further."

In the aftermath, there are other things to be considered. Saving their theatre is one of them. Although Brecht insists he didn't tell her "to go crawling," Volumnia brings the now triumphant Kozanka to the theatre. She even goes so far as to suggest that he ask the party hack to contribute a play. But, says Brecht, "There are limits to my guile." For a moment he resists adding his name to the list of those expressing unqualified support of the Socialist Unity party that Kozanka has been preparing. Volumnia insists he cannot treat this as if it were "some private quarrel." If he does, they'll "cancel our new theatre."

> We insist that you dissociate yourself from all counterrevolutionary machinations and congratulate—yes, congratulate—the government on its victory over the putschists and provocateurs.

Kozanka goes further: "And now your signature. Or else!"

And so Brecht writes the famous letter to Ulbricht. In the first two paragraphs he criticizes the measures taken by the government as premature. In the third he proclaims his solidarity with that same government. He knows, as Volumnia tells him, that "they'll cross out the critical paragraphs and trumpet the solidarity until you die of shame." But he lamely insists he has a carbon copy, and that no one will dare to censor him. Never mind, suggests Erwin, "even uncut it's feeble." Brecht sends one copy to the Central Committee, the other to "friends in the West for safekeeping."

PODULLA: Boss, they'll say we're sitting on the fence.

BOSS: Answer, what better seat have you to offer? . . .

LITTHENNER: Won't we feel ashamed of ourselves for the rest of our lives?

180

BOSS: I feel ashamed already.

And the Boss, Brecht, packs up his papers, takes his cap, and goes off to the house he has rented on a lake, "bowed down with guilt."

That Volumnia's prediction accurately reflects what happened is today well known. Brecht had been too clever. The June 21 issue of the East German *Neues Deutschland* carried a brief mention of his letter to Ulbricht, quoting only the last sentence: "I feel the need to express to you at this moment my attachment to the Socialist Unity Party." In Western eyes, Brecht had become, as the Swiss journalist Gody Suter later noted, "a loyal henchman of the executioners." Suter went on to refer to how Brecht would eagerly pull "the tattered original of that letter, that he had obviously shown to many people, from his pocket."

Grass's Brecht is something less than a complete villain and something less—a great deal less—than an even potential hero. In a sense, he is what Martin Esslin has referred to as the "image of the self-castrated German intellectual." His dilemma was Grass's and any writer's dilemma: to become *engagé*—to speak out at a time when silence was both expeditious and possible, to put one's talents at the service of one's political or social convictions, or to remain above the battle, secure (or perhaps not so secure) in the belief that in the long run the artist contributes more by doing what he does best than by engaging in the day-to-day play of political affairs.

Perhaps more than Grass intended, *The Plebeians* makes Brecht not merely a complex but a sympathetic character. It reflects intriguingly and with an entirely appropriate irony a superb and incisive grasp of the Brechtian canon. (It would be interesting indeed to see, let us say, *Galileo* staged by Grass.) Beyond this, however, it explores with intelligence and imagination, if somewhat diffusedly and with excessive intellectuality, the role of the artist in our or any other time. It is this, not any theatrical gossip-column qualities, that lends it its long-term interest.

CONCLUSION

In an interview some years ago, Harold Pinter was asked to explain the ambiguity that pervades his plays. To explain not so much what it "meant," but why it was there in the first place; why the relationships between characters, what they mean, what they are doing, were almost always subject to conjecture. Why there was always an element of doubt. "The thing is not necessarily either true or false," he responded, "it can be both true and false."

If it is the element of doubt, of gray, in Pinter's plays that lends them much of their fascination, it is the absence of doubt—the unwillingness to entertain its possibility—that cripples many, perhaps most, of the plays in the theatre of controversy. For to exclude doubt too often means to exclude the very conflict that is the essence of drama. Pursuing his polemic, the playwright all too frequently becomes its prisoner.

It is not necessarily that he becomes disingenuous—*Inquest* is the only play of the nearly two dozen I have been discussing that seems to me to approach that. And to fail largely because of it, sacrificing the very real drama of the Rosenberg case in favor of a cheap play on the emotions. Curiously, the reaction to the very book on which Donald Freed's play was based— Walter and Miriam Schneir's *Invitation to an Inquest*—suggests not only why it largely succeeded but why *Inquest* and many similar theatrical polemics do not.

The reviewers were as divided over the case made by the book—over what it "proved"—as the American public had been over the trial itself. One, Fred Cook, found that it cast doubts

183

on the Rosenbergs' guilt "to a point of proof that cannot be ignored." Another, however, felt just the opposite. The book, concluded Phoebe Adams, "has the effect of persuading me that they were guilty—a thing I have never been certain of before." Whatever else, the book made you *think*.

The play, on the other hand, failed almost precisely because it never for an instant permitted the audience to entertain the possibility that there had been, still is, a question concerning the Rosenbergs. In sacrificing reason to emotionalism, it simultaneously sacrificed the possibility of convincing anyone of anything. It is only when men think that they truly change; only when plays cause them to think that they bring about change.

Clearly, I'm not talking about the agit-prop of the 30s or the street theatre of today, both of which seek not so much to convince an audience by the marshaling of "facts," selected, filtered, or otherwise, but to move it to recognition and response—a recognition and response more often evoked through the immediacy of the images than through verbal polemics. Guerrilla theatre is one thing, plays like *Inquest, The Deputy, The Trial of the Catonsville Nine* another.

It is precisely because they are so different that the play that acknowledges the possibility—the certainty—of doubt, of those areas of gray, is more likely to succeed. Succeed both as play and as polemic. It is why Heinar Kipphardt's *In the Matter of J. Robert Oppenheimer*, hardly a good play, is so much more effective as political theatre than *Inquest, Vietnam Discourse*, or *We Bombed in New Haven*. Depicting Oppenheimer as troubled, torn by doubt, even partly culpable in his own undoing—anything but a plaster saint—and his accusers not as villains but as men convinced, albeit mistakenly, of the truth of what they did, it acknowledges the areas of ambiguity in the thoughts and actions of men. In acknowledging them, it reminds us that conscience, motivation, and moral complexity, not black-and-white actions, are the essence of life and their embodiment the essence of good theatre, whether political or otherwise.

Jules Feiffer pinpointed the problem when he said: "I don't mean one of my characters to be spokesman for the writer, walking frontstage and saying, 'I know the trouble with us, the trouble with us is . . .' That's just too simple-minded. A character can't just stand on stage and tell us what's right and wrong. . . . What can happen is that character can stand on stage and argue from various fixed points, none of which are absolutely right. And by listening (you are forced to listen if the arguments are interesting enough) the point of view emerges for the audience."

None of which are absolutely right. This is the key. Not, of course, the key to all the plays that have been considered, but the key to most of those that have failed. Failed to convince, failed to change minds, failed to move, failed to work as theatre. How much stronger, for instance, would Hochhuth's *The Deputy* have been had he explored the motives—the soul, the conscience, the almost undoubted periods of indecision—of Pius XII and *then* challenged and refuted him for his alleged indifference, moral cowardice, expediency, sin? How much stronger would Weiss's *Vietnam Discourse* have been had he, instead of setting up straw men, puppets, and caricatures, shown us what most fair-minded men would agree were individuals who, at a given moment in time, were acting out of something—mistaken though it was—that went beyond greed, imperialism, and capitalist self-aggrandizement? They almost certainly were wrong. It is difficult to believe they were quite as evilly motivated as Weiss insists. It is equally difficult not to believe that *Vietnam Discourse* would have been a far more effective play and a far more effective polemic had he permitted his "capitalists" some sense of conviction, some sense that they were acting rightly, rather than insisting on a monochromatic parade of good guys and bad, caricatures who can speak only to the converted.

We are involved with something more than a simple question of credibility—though credibility is certainly a factor. Brecht asked the question: "How can the unfree, ignorant man of our century, with his thirst for freedom and his hunger for knowledge, how can the tortured and heroic, abused and ingenious, changeable and world-changing man of this great and ghastly century obtain his own theatre, which will help him to master the world and himself?"

185

How indeed? Well, certainly no more through one-sided theatrical propaganda pieces ("right" or "wrong") than through the double-think of many a press secretary's handout or presidential news conference. He can "master himself" only if he is brought to look within himself, to see what there is within him, within his species, that causes a Vietnam, an Auschwitz, a McCarthy witch hunt, a persecution of the Indians, to happen.

If it is made black-and-white, he conceivably may believe the playwright for the moment, but it will be a futile exercise: Oh, look how bad we—or some—mortals be! But, somewhere, he knows it is not black-and-white. He knows it just because he knows his own life: how he cuts corners—and men—how he cheats and takes the easy, the expedient way; how he seldom really gives a damn about anything that fails to touch *him* directly. And he knows that very little of it is nearly as calculated and clear-cut as the polemical playwright too often suggests. He knows he may be partially corrupt, but he also knows his motives, the bases for his actions, are far more complex than the playwright allows for. He knows that men—a Hitler perhaps aside—and nations seldom have been evil incarnate. If he is intelligent enough to want to influence, he is very likely too intelligent to *be* influenced by most of the oversimplified, black-and-white plays that pass for political theatre today. He may have his prejudices catered to or confirmed; he may have some kind of political orgasm at their satisfaction. He may even wind up enjoying himself. That he'll walk out of the theatre thinking any differently seems altogether unlikely.

It is not a coincidence that the best polemics have also been the best plays. *The Basic Training of Pavlo Hummel* works—has impact—not through a denunciation of the American role in Vietnam, but because it recognizes that war *does* have a lure for men, that they kill and are willing to kill for complex and varied reasons. Those reasons may make no sense, but they are there. And, regrettably, they probably will continue to be there. David Rabe shows them for the aberration they are, shows war for the aberration it is. He refuses, however, to make them the exclusive preserve of one time or one nation. In doing so, he indicts not just America but Americans, not just Americans but most of mankind. For most of mankind *will* pull triggers, drop

186

bombs, mine harbors, given what they take to be the right occasion.

O'Casey's *The Silver Tassie* becomes a good play—an effective antiwar statement—only in the second act, in that scene in the "jagged and lacerated ruin" of a monastery in the war zone. It is there that it relies on images, on poetry, and on irony to stir the audience to an abhorrence of war and the men who cause it, only to have other men fight it. Transmuted nearly to the maudlin, certainly to the overstated, in the remaining two acts, the play loses both dimension and power. What remains is the image, the impression, not the blatant insistence.

In a long essay on *The Deputy*, the Swiss critic Rolf C. Zimmermann noted that, "first and foremost, the language of the polemicist is an instrument of demonstration, not one that mirrors itself and its author. The polemicist is not an artist but a demonstrator. It is almost inevitable—when a dramatic form of demonstration is involved—that he will allow his main character to become a demonstrator too. . . . And while with poetry the extent of its cause is irrelevant, with the polemic—precisely for the sake of the cause—it is a sign of its quality."

Throughout, I have suggested that the "cause" is best served when it is least obviously seen to be served—when the service is least heavy-handed. When, on occasion, two sides (not the same thing as saying "both sides," for there are usually more than two) are shown. In a review of *The Crucible*, Harold Hobson asserted: "What Acton said was the duty of the historian is no less that of the dramatist: to be fair to the other side."* I seriously doubt that. I do, however, think that the dramatist, the political dramatist, will be most effective when he acknowledges that there *is* another side and gives it at least a little stage room. Then he can shoot it down however he wishes. Refutation, disputation, contention—all these are inherently more dramatic, inherently more convincing, than simple assertion, simple insistence.

Political theatre has gone through various phases. One can trace it back through the American 30s, Shaw, Shakespeare, and far, far beyond—to the beginnings of recorded drama, if he

The Sunday Times (London), 14 November, 1954, p.11.

187

wishes. In the West, particularly in America, it has been a peculiarly quixotic thing. Years ago, reading Harold Clurman's *The Fervent Years* (his account of the rise and fall of the Group Theatre), I came upon his description of the 1935 opening of Clifford Odets's *Waiting for Lefty:*

> When the audience at the end of the play responded to the militant question from the stage—"Well, what's the answer?"— with a spontaneous roar of "Strike! Strike!" it was something more than a tribute to the play's effectiveness. . . . Our youth had found its voice. The audience was delirious. It stormed the stage.

There were people on the stage—if not exactly storming it—during the Living Theatre's 1968 return to the United States. I have seen an audience at the off-Off Broadway Theatre Genesis roused, with techniques I can only compare with those used at the Nuremberg rallies, to a stamping of feet and rhythmic chanting of "Power to the People!" I could not believe, in either case, that "our youth had found its voice." (I don't think they had at *Waiting for Lefty* either, but that's another matter.) At most, they had found an echo. At worst, they were being used.

That seems to me to be the problem of political, polemical, protest theatre—call it what you will—in the future. If it is to have a role, it must lead, not follow. It's all very well to explore what Pius XII did or didn't do during World War II; all very well to beat our breasts over American mistreatment of the Indians; all very well for black playwrights to indict white Americans for their inexcusable past actions and inaction. It is all very well to say the Vietnam War is wrong, was wrong from the beginning, that the Nazis' attempted genocide of the Jews almost defies explanation, and that the USSR, declining to acknowledge Trotsky, declines to acknowledge a major, perhaps pivotal, figure in her history.

But, in the end, what does it all come down to; what does it influence; what does it change? As I suggested at the beginning, I'm not at all sure the theatre can fill this role—be an agent of

188

influence, an agent for change. Eric Bentley may be right when he says: "God help any regime—and God help any rebellion— that depends heavily on its artists! They are on the whole, not a dangerous lot, as Plato thought, but a useless lot."* I do not, not by any means, think they are useless. I do wonder, however, if they may not become so if they fail to recognize that life has become far too complex to take a placard—or a point of view—make it into a play, and expect it to become a successful polemic. Nothing's quite that simple—not anymore.

*The Theatre of Commitment (New York: Atheneum, 1967), p. 123.

189

BIBLIOGRAPHY

The Plays

Berrigan, Daniel. *The Trial of the Catonsville Nine.* Boston: Beacon Press, 1970.

Feiffer, Jules. *God Bless. Plays and Players,* January, 1969, pp. 35-50.

——. *Little Murders.* New York: Random House, 1968.

Freed, Donald. *Inquest.* New York: Hill and Wang, A Spotlight Dramabook, 1970.

Gordone, Charles. *No Place to Be Somebody.* Indianapolis and New York: Bobbs-Merrill, 1969.

Grass, Günter. *The Plebeians Rehearse the Uprising: A German Tragedy.* Translated by Ralph Manheim. New York: Harcourt, Brace and World, 1966.

Heller, Joseph. *We Bombed in New Haven.* New York: Alfred A. Knopf, 1968.

Hochhuth, Rolf. *The Deputy.* Translated by Richard and Clara Winston. New York: Grove Press, 1964.

——. *Soldiers.* Translated by Robert David MacDonald. New York: Grove Press, 1968.

Kipphardt, Heinar. *In the Matter of J. Robert Oppenheimer.* Translated by Ruth Speirs. New York: Hill and Wang, A Spotlight Dramabook, 1968.

Kopit, Arthur. *Indians.* New York: Hill and Wang, A Spotlight Dramabook, 1969.

Miller, Arthur. *The Crucible.* New York: The Viking Press, 1953.

O'Brien, Conor Cruise. *Murderous Angels: A Political Tragedy and Comedy in Black and White.* Boston: Little, Brown, An Atlantic Monthly Press Book, 1968.

O'Casey, Sean. *Three More Plays: The Silver Tassie, Purple Dust, Red Roses for Me.* Introduction by J. C. Trewin. New York: St. Martin's Press, 1965.

Rabe, David. *The Basic Training of Pavlo Hummel. Scripts,* November 1971, pp. 56-92.

Shaw, Robert. *The Man in the Glass Booth.* New York: Grove Press, 1968.

Weiss, Peter. *The Investigation.* English version by Jon Swan and Ulu Grosbard. New York: Atheneum, 1966.

———. *Trotsky in Exile.* Translated by Geoffrey Skelton. New York: Atheneum, 1972.

———. *Two Plays: Song of the Lusitanian Bogey and Discourse on . . . Vietnam.* Translated by Lee Baxandall and Geoffrey Skelton respectively. New York: Atheneum, 1970.

Wesley, Richard. *The Black Terror. Scripts,* December 1971, pp. 71-101.

General

Anderson, Michael, Guicharnaud, Jacques, and others. *Crowell's Handbook of Contemporary Drama.* New York: Thomas Y. Crowell, 1971.

Atkinson, Brooks. *Broadway.* New York: Macmillan, 1970.

Bentley, Eric. *The Playwright As Thinker: A Study of Drama in Modern Times.* New York: Meridian, 1955.

———. *The Theatre of Commitment and Other Essays.* New York: Atheneum, 1967.

Berrigan, Daniel. *Night Flight to Hanoi.* New York: Macmillan, 1968.

Berrigan, Philip. *Prison Journals of a Priest Revolutionary.* Compiled and edited by Vincent McGee. Introduction by Daniel Berrigan. New York: Holt, Rinehart and Winston, 1970.

Brustein, Robert. *The Theatre of Revolt: An Approach to Modern Drama.* Boston: Atlantic-Little, Brown, 1964.

Bucher, Lloyd M. *Bucher: My Story.* With Mark Rascovich. Garden City, N.Y.: Doubleday, 1970.

Casey, William Van Etten, S.J., and Nobile, Philip, eds. *The Berrigans.* New York: Avon Books, 1971.

Clurman, Harold. *The Naked Image: Observations on the Modern Theatre.* New York: Macmillan, 1966.

Deutscher, Isaac. *The Prophet Outcast: Trotsky: 1929-1940.* New York: Oxford University Press, 1963.

Esslin, Martin. *Brecht: The Man and His Work.* Garden City, N.Y.: Doubleday, Anchor Books, 1961.

———. *Reflections: Essays on Modern Theatre.* Garden City, N.Y.: Doubleday, Anchor Books, 1971.

Fall, Bernard B. *The Two Viet-Nams: A Political and Military Analysis.* 2nd rev. ed. New York: Frederick A. Praeger, 1967.

Fischer, Louis. *The Life of Lenin.* New York: Harper and Row, 1964.

Georgiyev, N. *Soviet Union Today.* Translated by Jim Riordan. Moscow: Progress Publishers, 1971.

Gray, Ronald. *Bertolt Brecht.* New York: Grove Press, 1961.

Hilton, Ian. *Peter Weiss: A Search for Affinities.* London: Oswald Wolff, 1970.

Hyde, H. Montgomery. *Stalin: The History of a Dictator.* New York: Farrar, Straus and Giroux, 1972.

Kerr, Walter. *God on the Gymnasium Floor and Other Theatrical Adventures.* New York: Simon and Schuster, 1971.

———. *Thirty Plays Hath November: Pain and Pleasure in the Contemporary Theatre.* New York: Simon and Schuster, 1969.

Kott, Jan. *Theatre Notebook: 1947-1967.* Translated by Boleslaw Taborski. Garden City, N.Y.: Doubleday, 1968.

Krupskaya, N. K. *Reminiscences of Lenin.* Translated by Bernard Isaacs. New York: International Publishers, 1970.

Lahr, John. *Up Against the Fourth Wall: Essays on Modern Theatre.* New York: Grove Press, 1970.

McCann, Sean, ed. *The Story of the Abbey Theatre.* London: The New English Library, Four Square Books, 1967.

Murarka, Dev. *The Soviet Union.* New York: Walker, 1971.

Naumann, Bernd. *Auschwitz.* Introduction by Hannah Arendt. New York: Frederick A. Praeger, 1966.

Payne, Robert. *The Rise and Fall of Stalin.* New York: Simon and Schuster, 1965.

Schneir, Walter and Miriam. *Invitation to an Inquest: A New Look at the Rosenberg-Sobell Case.* Garden City, N.Y.: Doubleday, 1965.

Shaw, Robert. *The Man in the Glass Booth* (novel). New York: Harcourt, Brace and World, 1967.

Starkey, Marion L. *The Devil in Massachusetts: A Modern Enquiry into the Salem Witch Trials.* New York: Alfred A. Knopf, 1949; Garden City, N.Y.: Doubleday, Anchor Books, 1969.

Sukhanov, N. N. *The Russian Revolution 1917: Eyewitness Account.* Edited, abridged, and translated by Joel Carmichael. New York: Oxford University Press, 1955.

Trotsky, Leon. *The Essential Trotsky.* New York: Barnes and Noble, 1963.

Tynan, Kenneth. *Curtains.* New York: Atheneum, 1961.

Ulam, Adam B. *The Bolsheviks.* New York: Macmillan, 1965.

Wager, Walter, ed. *The Playwrights Speak.* New York: Dell, 1968.

Weales, Gerald. *American Drama Since World War II.* New York: Harcourt, Brace and World, 1962.

——, ed. *The Crucible: Text and Criticism.* New York: The Viking Press, The Viking Critical Library, 1971.

Weiss, Peter. "An Open Letter to the *Literaturnaya Gazeta.*" Frankfurt am Main: Suhrkamp Verlag, 1971.

Wolfe, Bertram D. *Three Who Made a Revolution: A Biographical History.* Rev. ed. New York: Dell, 1964.

Zahn, Gordon. *German Catholics and Hitler's Wars: A Study in Social Control.* New York: Sheed and Ward, 1962.